CONTENTS

INTRODUCTION

· · · · · · · · · · · · · · · · ·

This 15-month guide has been designed and written to give
a concise and accessible insight into both the nature of your
star sign and the year ahead. Divided into two main sections,
the first section of this guide will give you an overview of your
character in order to help you understand how you think,
perceive the world and interact with others and – perhaps just
as importantly – why. You'll soon see that your zodiac sign
is not just affected by a few stars in the sky, but by planets,
elements, and a whole host of other factors, too.

The second section of this guide is made up of daily forecasts.
Use these to increase your awareness of what might appear on
your horizon so that you're better equipped to deal with the
days ahead. While this should never be used to dictate your life,
it can be useful to see how your energies might be affected or
influenced, which in turn can help you prepare for what life
might throw your way.

By the end of these 15 months, these two sections should
have given you a deeper understanding and awareness of
yourself and, in turn, the world around you. There are never
any definite certainties, but with an open mind you will find
guidance for what might be, and learn to take more control of
your own destiny.

THE CHARACTER OF THE SCALES

. . . .

Symbolised by Scales and flying on the element of air, Libra is a sign of grace and harmony. It is the serene dove carrying an olive branch that offers peace to the zodiac calendar. Librans themselves often act as a cooling breeze that can placate the most heated of situations with diplomacy and charm. Ruled by the bright and beautiful Venus, their exquisite good looks can leave admirers breathless. Whether they are breaking the Internet like Kim Kardashian or stunning the screen like Brigitte Bardot, Librans have characteristically balanced features that can become their fortune. Whilst personal appearance is important to them, Librans are also skilled at creating beauty too. Therefore, the scales might be tipped in their favour if they wish to pursue a creative career in art, architecture, fashion or design.

Born at the start of autumn with a unique cardinal and air combination, Librans are among some of the most pioneering thinkers. Whether people agree with their way of thinking or not, their cardinal attitude has them actively striving for what they believe to be fair. It is, in fact, the one sign that can lay claim to the two, and only, female prime ministers in the UK; Theresa May and Margaret Thatcher. However, rising to the top of their profession can be lonely for Librans, who are not content to have only their shadow for company. Born in the seventh house that focuses on finding a partner, Librans will need to find the eggs to their bacon, the pen to their paper, the weights to their scales in order to personally find the peace and beauty that they are so intent on bringing to others.

Your Horoscope 2021

....

Libra

24 September – 23 October

igloobooks

igloobooks

Published in 2020
by Igloo Books Ltd
Cottage Farm
Sywell
NN6 0BJ
www.igloobooks.com

0820 001
2 4 6 8 10 9 7 5 3 1
ISBN 978-1-83852-321-3

Written by Belinda Campbell and Denise Evans

Cover design by Simon Parker
Edited by Bobby Newlyn-Jones

Printed and manufactured in China

SCALES

The scales of justice are an enduring symbol used by courts and legal systems the world over, which makes it the perfect representation for fair-thinking Librans. Whether they're working as lawyers or campaigning as activists, they often feel strongly about their need to rectify any injustices – whether the issues affect them directly or not. The world should get ready for the weight of Librans, as the try their best to strike a balance for everyone, and civil rights activist Mahatma Gandhi is the perfect example. Originally a barrister, he led a non-violence movement towards the ideals of peace and freedom that inspired, and continues to inspire, millions of people. Librans tend to like to weigh up all their options before making decisions, so don't expect any hasty judgements. Whether it's deciding between two potential partners or between the beef and chicken, Librans can be plagued with indecision and may evade picking a side to avoid upsetting anyone. Finding equilibrium can be difficult, but these careful and considered types will usually judge fairly. Life is a balancing act for everyone, but especially so for Librans.

VENUS

One of the brightest objects in the sky, the beautiful Venus is Libra's ruling planet. Guided by the planet of love and born in the seventh house of relationships, Librans may feel destined to find companionship and settle down in life. Venus is the hottest planet in the solar system and named after the Roman goddess of beauty, which may well be why Librans have such a reputation for being so attractive. Whilst beauty is in the eye of the beholder, there will typically be something aesthetic about Librans that catches the admiration of potential partners – whether it's their charming wit or the beauty that they can capture in a poem, painting or floral arrangement. Venus is associated with fertility, which could link to every Libran's love of being outdoors, as well as their positive energy that feeds off external stimulation. Spending quality time soaking up the beauty of nature and stargazing to try and spot their shining planet of Venus may be where Librans find their one true love.

ELEMENTS, MODES AND POLARITIES

Each sign is made up of a unique combination of three defining groups: elements, modes and polarities. Each of these defining parts can manifest themselves in good and bad ways and none should be seen as a positive or a negative – including the polarities! Just like a jigsaw puzzle, piecing these groups together can help illuminate why each sign has certain characteristics and help us find a balance.

ELEMENTS

Fire: Dynamic and adventurous, signs with fire in them can be extroverted. Others are naturally drawn to them because of the positive light they give off, as well as their high levels of energy and confidence.

Earth: Signs with the earth element are steady and driven with their ambitions. They make for a solid friend, parent or partner due to their grounded influence and nurturing nature.

Air: The invisible element that influences each of the other elements significantly, air signs will provide much-needed perspective to others with their fair thinking, verbal skills and key ideas.

Water: Warm in the shallows and freezing as ice. This mysterious element is essential to the growth of everything around it, through its emotional depth and empathy.

MODES

Cardinal: Pioneers of the calendar, cardinal signs jump-start each season and are the energetic go-getters.

Fixed: Marking the middle of the calendar, fixed signs firmly denote and value steadiness and reliability.

Mutable: As the seasons end, the mutable signs adapt and give themselves over gladly to the promise of change.

POLARITIES

Positive: Typically extroverted, positive signs take physical action and embrace outside stimulus in their life.

Negative: Usually introverted, negative signs value emotional development and experiencing life from the inside out.

LIBRA IN BRIEF

The table below shows the key attributes of Librans.
Use it for quick reference and to understand more about this fascinating sign.

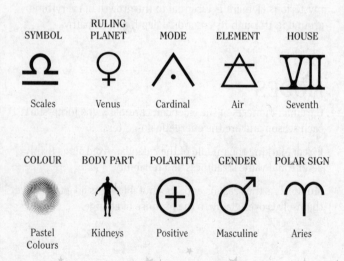

SYMBOL	RULING PLANET	MODE	ELEMENT	HOUSE
Scales	Venus	Cardinal	Air	Seventh

COLOUR	BODY PART	POLARITY	GENDER	POLAR SIGN
Pastel Colours	Kidneys	Positive	Masculine	Aries

ROMANTIC RELATIONSHIPS

. . . .

Look straight ahead because it's nothing but blue skies for Librans in love. Filled from the inside out with beauty and charm, thanks to the influence of their ruling planet Venus, the allure of ever-graceful Librans is felt by many. Appearances can be important to them, so they will usually try to look nice for their partners and will appreciate it when their partners do so in return; slouching around in pyjamas or holding on to that pizza-stained sweatshirt will not go down well with elegant Librans. These artistic types will usually have exceptional taste and their style will always be impeccable, so whether they're blessed in the looks department or not there will likely be something visually appealing that catches the attention of others.

Finding that special someone can feel essential for Librans to feel whole. Being alone can feel as much fun as a see-saw with only one person on it, which could not be worse for these seekers of balance. Whether it's through their beauty or charm, Librans will actively seek out relationships and may discover that love finds them frequently owing to their airy, socialite way. Belonging to the seventh house in the zodiac calendar that represents relationships and contracts, wedding bells are likely to chime loudly and clearly for loved-up Librans. In fact, their big white day will usually be planned to perfection with white doves released on cue.

Being in a partnership is where Librans usually feel most content, with someone by their side as constant stimulation. They seek peace and harmony, and are experts at being tactful and at finding compromise. Despite all this, their relationships will not be without some conflicts. When Librans start to pick a fight, it is a sure sign that they are really unhappy about something. Overall, however, these pacifists are most definitely lovers and not fighters, so hopefully talking problems through openly should help them get back to marital bliss.

ARIES: COMPATIBILITY 5/5

A polarity is complementary for any star-sign pairing. For an Arian and Libran, this can be a real yin and yang kind of love. The Libran's air element can make the Arian's flames burn that much brighter. The Libran is best known for bringing harmony and balance into the world, and can make an ideal partner for the often-combative Arian. In this partnership of opposites, each can learn from the other in areas that they are lacking, with the Libran encouraging the Arian to communicate, and the Arian inspiring the Libran into action.

TAURUS: COMPATIBILITY 4/5

Both ruled by the planet Venus, the love that a Taurean and Libran share can be a thing of beauty. Their shared appreciation of culture and aesthetics will have romance blooming quickly. Wedding bells will ring in both the Taurean and Libran's ears, and planning for the big day will begin sooner rather than later. The Libran's airy indecisiveness can be a point of contention for the grounded Taurean, and these two won't be without their disagreements. However, the Libran's diplomacy will help to resolve issues and have them striving for harmony once more.

GEMINI: COMPATIBILITY 3/5

With Libra ruled by the planet of love, Venus, and Gemini by the planet of communication, Mercury, this partnership should be founded on affection and understanding. The debate-loving Geminian and peace-seeking Libran will likely have their conflicts. If love troubles do arise, these two will have a good chance of having the verbal skills and creative thinking to work out their issues. Both can have trouble making up their minds, however. The Libran's cardinal instinct usually sets in to help make the course of action clear, much to the delight of the mutable Geminian.

CANCER: COMPATIBILITY 3/5

Ruled by the planet of love and the emotions of the Moon, the romance between a Libran and Cancerian can read like an epic poem. The Libran's love for aesthetics will be particularly attractive to the creative Crab, and encourage many artistic endeavours. The home that these two could build together might well be a thing of beauty and harmony. Both cardinal characters, the Libran and Cancerian match each other's energetic attitudes, but may fight for power in the relationship. Whilst their introvert and extrovert tendencies could clash, the Libran's search for peace could help make this relationship last.

LEO: COMPATIBILITY 4/5

Sitting two places apart on the calendar, a Libran and Leonian can share a compatible partnership. The Libran is an expert in diplomacy, so will likely be able to handle the more dramatic moments in this love affair without bruising the Leonian's ego. Love with the Leonian can be a roller coaster, fun but also consisting of ups and downs. The Libran, symbolised by scales, will hopefully bring a balance to the relationship that the reliable Leonian will appreciate. Ruled by the Sun and Venus, the Leonian and Libran are capable of forming a relationship that is filled with warmth and love.

VIRGO: COMPATIBILITY 3/5

Both advocates of diplomacy and justice, a Libran and Virgoan's love should be fair and true. If these two make any vows together, they will take them very seriously. However, it is not all contracts and scales in this relationship, as the Mercury-inspired Virgoan and Venus-ruled Libran could both have a shared love of beauty and crafts. A date night at a gallery or the theatre could be perfect for the art-loving Virgoan and Libran couple. The Libran will have plenty of ideas, and the practical Virgoan could be the one that helps make those fancies a reality.

LIBRA: COMPATIBILITY 5/5

The love between two Librans can be sheer bliss. As a creative coupling, they will be each other's muses and inspire one another to bring beauty into the relationship. This is in no way a shallow meeting of minds, as these two great thinkers share air as their element and breathe with ideas and intellect. This luxury-loving pair will enjoy delicious dinners and gorgeous gifts, but they should be wary of overindulgence. Overall, the two Librans should easily find the balance and harmony that they both strive for in this partnership of true equals.

SCORPIO: COMPATIBILITY 2/5

When the planets align for a Scorpian and Libran, the combination of loving Venus, passionate Mars and powerful Pluto can make for an intimate and stimulating love affair. The emotions of the Scorpian and the mindfulness of the Libran can make for a harmonious pairing, so long as they are both on the same page. The Libran can seem superficial to the deep-feeling Scorpian, but thankfully the Libran's charm and diplomacy can help calm any troubled waters if they fail to understand one another. This love won't be without conflicts, but it could be loyal and long lasting.

SAGITTARIUS: COMPATIBILITY 4/5

With compatible ruling planets of Jupiter and Venus, a Sagittarian and Libran could be very lucky in love together. Their complementing elements of fire and air will no doubt spark a highly passionate union, full of excitement and intimacy. They are both brimming with positive energy, so should have no problem keeping up with their packed social schedules. The tactful Libran and sometimes blunt Sagittarian could clash if their ideas of commitment don't match, but they have a good chance of working out their differences and happily moving forwards together. Many adventures await.

CAPRICORN: COMPATIBILITY 1/5

A firm-footed Capricornian and high-spirited Libran could have little shared ground and may struggle to strike a balance in love. Yet a relationship should not be ruled out entirely. Born in the seventh house of relationships, the Libran may struggle if the Capricornian, born in the tenth house of careers, puts work before love, so reaching a compromise here will be essential for a happy union. It could be hard to find equality in this earth-and-air match when the differences are so plentiful, however, their commitment could well outweigh any differences.

AQUARIUS: COMPATIBILITY 5/5

It can be a whirlwind romance when an Aquarian and Libran fall in love. Ruled by Venus and Uranus, this may well be a rebellious or radical type of relationship. The cardinal Libran is quick to come up with ideas, while the Aquarian's fixed mode makes it possible to bring them to life. Teamwork really is dreamwork for this outgoing positive couple. The ideals of the Aquarian paired with the Libran's sense of righteousness can form a couple that will break down boundaries and create brand-new rules to make a utopic future.

PISCES: COMPATIBILITY 2/5

Whilst an enigmatic Piscean and suave Libran might be charmed by one another, theirs is a love that could struggle to reach fruition. The cardinal Libran is more likely to be the initiator in the relationship than the mutable Piscean, however, both can be struck with an inability to make decisions. This can leave them treading water, neither sinking nor swimming. The Libran will be attracted to the artistic side of the creative Piscean, and the Piscean is likely to flourish under the Libran's enthusiastic encouragement. If a balance can be found between the Libran's extrovert and the Piscean's introvert natures, romance is possible.

FAMILY AND FRIENDS

. . . .

Librans are friends to all. These diplomats may indeed be the peacekeepers in their circle of friends and family, although they are unlikely to take any sides and would rather remain neutral. Ultimate peace providers and avoiders of aggression, Librans long to bypass conflict, which can mean that they sacrifice too much for the sake of a quiet life. Whilst letting bossy Leonian friends choose the film on movie night may not seem like a big deal, Librans should avoid compromising what is truly important to them. They can sometimes be pushovers, but allowing their friends and family to walk all over them will clash with their inherent need for equality. Therefore, they should try to not be too docile in relationships and be confident with pushing back or saying no when it matters.

Being friends with light-hearted Librans can be a complete joy. They are sure to have an uplifting effect on their friends and family, whether it's putting the world to rights over a cup of coffee with Virgoans or persuading their homebody Cancerian friends to come out partying with them into the wee hours. At times, Librans can be a little flaky and may fail to do what they said they would. However, they often make up for their unreliability by showering friends and family with beautiful gifts, large and small, thoughtful and expensive. If Librans ever find themselves short of money, they will instead be generous with their time and love – the value of which their family and friends are sure to be grateful for.

Whether it's visiting free galleries, starting a book club or getting the best seats in the house for that stunning new show, arty Librans will probably be the refined comrades that keep their friends up to date with all the latest art and cultural affairs. A visit to a Libran house might be like stepping straight into a gallery, as it is bound to be filled with beautiful objects and design. Taureans, also ruled by Venus, will be more than happy to stop round for a glass of fine wine or two, and the attention to beautiful detail will also not go unnoticed by Virgoans.

When it comes to family, Librans can thrive in any environment that involves a partnership, so parenting may come naturally to them. Whilst they will enjoy spoiling their children, they will also be keen to instil the importance of sharing and playing fairly with others. Libran offspring might have the latest toys, but they'll need to play nicely if they want to hold on to them. Generous Librans will always prefer to be sympathetic to their children and may shy away from disciplining any bad behaviour, which can obviously be problematic. Learning how to take on the role of both the good cop and the bad cop will be beneficial in creating a balanced family unit.

MONEY AND CAREERS

....

Being a particular star sign will not dictate certain types of career, but it can help identify potential areas for thriving in. Conversely, to succeed in the workplace, it is just as important to understand strengths and weaknesses to achieve career and financial goals.

Whilst balance is key for Librans, balancing money might be a bit of a struggle for them. Tempted to choose the most beautiful things in life, tickets to the opera whilst wearing that new designer outfit for example, budgets may fly out of the window in the pursuit of beauty. Despite being great thinkers, these lovers of luxury may not have a flair for funds. Making an effort to sit down and work out their financial affairs, or perhaps even paying someone else to do it, could be essential for Librans to stay out of their overdrafts, while still being able to enjoy the occasional treat.

With an innate sense of both beauty and justice, careers in design or law could be two potential fields that Librans may flourish in. They are known for their great taste and glamour, so choosing a career where aesthetics are important, such as fashion, theatre or beauty, could be where they are naturally drawn. Walking down the catwalk, like famous Libran model Bella Hadid, or designing clothes, like Donna Karan, may be dream jobs. Alternatively, the aesthetic of language or music may be just as appealing for Librans if they are disinclined towards public image, with Oscar Wilde and T.S. Eliot ably demonstrating how words can create an equally rich and beautiful picture as graphic art, whilst Franz Liszt and Ray

Charles are fine examples of the spectrum of musical talent Librans could possess if so inclined. If the courthouse is more appealing than the catwalk, working in the justice system could be the perfect fit for diplomatic Librans. Working as judges, activists or lawyers, where Librans can contribute to restoring the balance of justice in the world, may be an ideal fit. Whether it's using their profile to make the world a better place, like Bob Geldof, or working directly to ensure fairness and justice is delivered, like Judge Judy, Librans can be found striving for a greater good. Whether in politics or show business, Librans can find themselves comfortable in the public eye, numbering presidents and Oscar-winners amongst their ranks. They love to entertain, making people happy sitting neatly next to their drive to make the world a better place for everyone.

Reasonable and cooperative, Librans can make for the fairest of bosses and will work hard to create a tranquil environment for their employees to thrive in. If their colleagues are feeling disgruntled, Librans will work hard at finding resolutions to fix the problem. They will likely not tolerate gossip or unfair behaviour in the workplace, and will quickly extinguish it if they catch wind of it. Whether it's managing an office of people or umpiring a sports game, the rulings of Librans should be fair and final.

As with family, colleagues cannot be chosen. Therefore, it can be advantageous to use star signs to learn about their key characteristics and discover the best ways of working together. Partnerships are integral to Librans, so finding kindred work colleagues can really help them take flight in their careers. With the same element of air, Geminians and Aquarians will connect with Librans on a thoughtful level, and can make inspiring and influential colleagues. Libran John Lennon and Geminian Paul McCartney are a great example of the dizzying heights of success that these two deep-thinkers can help each other reach.

HEALTH AND WELLBEING

. . . .

Finding serenity is essential to peaceful Librans, so stressful situations can be particularly damaging to them. At times, these high-flyers could start to feel detached from the people around them and their day-to-day routines, particularly if they live in a built-up area. A change of scenery may help Librans shed some of that restlessness. A walk to the top of a hill or to the beach, wherever their element of air can freely whip around them, can help restore calmness. Learning meditation is another technique that Librans could try to ease their worries, and they can even practise whilst commuting to work if they travel by train or bus. Breathing exercises are a particularly effective calming method, and are again quick and easy enough to practise whilst on the move. By taking regular deep breaths, at least three in a row, they should feel panic leave and rational thoughts return once more.

Librans are usually great thinkers. Yet whilst some will find answers quickly, others may get stuck in a painful mental state of constant indecision. Bouncing off ideas with colleagues or a partner is one reason why they always like to have company, as it makes finalising plans far easier for them. Such is their hatred of being the lone decision-maker, Librans may end up leaving it to fate by flipping a coin. However, they should remind themselves that they actually possess the rationality to make extremely sound judgements. Whilst they may argue that two heads are always better than one, being confident to make up their own minds may have the double benefit of helping them feel more comfortable with their own company. Although it is their preference, Librans will do well to realise that they don't necessarily need a partner for everything.

HEALTH AND WELLBEING

Music can be a powerful healer for Librans, whether they are the musician, like fellow Librans John Lennon and Bruce Springsteen, or whether they are the recipients. Simply listening to their favourite artists or an inspiring playlist after a hard day could help lift them. They may want to take their love for music one step further, by hitting the dance floor to blow off some steam. If Librans can't convince their friends to grab their dancing shoes and meet them at the club, then joining a dance class at a gym or studio could be a great way of regularly experiencing the joys of music and dance. Engaging in physical activities that combine both their love of socialising and music is a winning combination for Librans.

Libra

....

DAILY FORECASTS
for 2020

OCTOBER

. . . .

Thursday 1st

Happy Full Moon in Aries! It's happening in your house
of relationships so puts the focus here. Take some time to
examine your relationships. Which of them are in alignment
with you and which ones aren't? Where do you need to stand
up for yourself and where are you too demanding?

Friday 2nd

Venus, your planetary ruler, is entering your area of
transcendence, reflection and retreat. This will give you the
opportunity to make some adjustments, as the entire topic
might seem more compelling than before. If you take this
chance to integrate time for yourself into your routine, it will
help you to maintain more harmony and balance.

Saturday 3rd

Somebody you trust might provide a resource that helps you
on your path. It could be a retreat location, an online course
or something else that allows you to connect to your core and
the divine. Yoga might be a good thing to try, as it will connect
you with your body.

Sunday 4th

It's good that Sunday is here, and you can stay in bed as long
as you want or lounge about in your favourite pyjamas all day.
However, a surprise visitor could put your plans in jeopardy.
Why not invite them to relax with you? Who says pyjama
parties are only for night-time?

Monday 5th

Pluto, the agent of change, evolution and transformation, is turning direct. This means the recent deconstruction phase is over, and you can now pick up the pieces and build from scratch. You can also see what has been liberated and where you can evolve next. Be patient, time will tell.

Tuesday 6th

How about a holiday? Now that the significant work is done you can think about taking a break and exploring something different. It would be good to have some new experiences, as they can broaden your mind. Afterwards, you will either appreciate what you have or know what you are seeking.

Wednesday 7th

A look at your finances might bring surprising facts to the surface. Make sure the money you need is available to you, and avoid gambling. Help might be on the way, should that be required. You can count on a solution that leaves you in a comfortable space, although you might need to raid the piggy bank.

Thursday 8th

The Moon is entering your career and holiday sector, which will either bring a sense of tension or a sense of satisfaction. It might depend on how much you are now putting into fulfilling your vocation. If you have not made enough space yet, the desire to do so will be strong and undeniable.

. . . .

Friday 9th

It's another two-part day. Your mood will support your attempts at self-reflection, allowing you some relief. A struggle in your relationship might feel real, however. Avoid power struggles and talk lovingly with your partner. They might be stuck in a defensive mood, even though it's entirely unnecessary.

Saturday 10th

Venus is in a loving conversation with Uranus, which will allow you to share a secret. It might be a relief to finally talk about it. Once again, your vocation could be in conflict with your responsibilities. This might seem like a never-ending story, but it is actually letting you pursue your heart's desire.

Sunday 11th

Enough is enough. Some of your beliefs about family are up for another review. You show dedication and commitment, but what is the real definition of responsibility? Is it the same for everybody involved? You might need to make some adjustments here, so your new persona can be aligned with your conscientiousness.

Monday 12th

The universe provides a break from the recent demanding energies. You need to be out and about, meeting your friends, interacting in your social circles and feeling the spirit of the future knocking at your door. If your heart is all in, you know you're on the right path.

Tuesday 13th

Are you ready for some more intensity? The Sun is in dispute with Mars retrograde, which will leave you trying to find equilibrium between your needs and your partner's needs. One of your tasks in this life is to understand that you will only be able to give more if you honour your own needs first.

Wednesday 14th

Another Mercury retrograde is here, and it's happening in Scorpio. This spells intensity and depth, and most likely has a lot to do with your possessions or finances. You have the opportunity to set things up differently. That includes where your money comes from and what you spend it on.

Thursday 15th

The Sun is in friction with Pluto today, but you already know that change is for the greatest good. Embrace what's coming up and choose to change voluntarily. You'll have a much easier time if you do so. Ease any tension by dancing or walking with a friend.

Friday 16th

Here comes the New Moon in Libra. This year has already been intense, and when you look back you might find that you're no longer the person who began 2020. Who do you want to be, and what is the image you're aiming for? Set your intentions now.

Saturday 17th

You have a feeling that something might be amiss with your resources. If you trust your intuition, it will likely lead you in surprising directions. It's as if you're a detective following a lead. Remain optimistic though, and don't meet the trouble halfway.

Sunday 18th

This is the final square from the Sun to Saturn in your area of home and family. This is the final test to make sure your foundation is stable. Saturn is a tough but fair teacher, so rewards will be granted if you've done the necessary work.

Monday 19th

The beliefs you find to be true are in conflict with your current relationship, or at least with the way you've been acting in that relationship. You'll be asked to either change your behaviour or walk away completely. Be sure to choose love and fairness.

Tuesday 20th

You're about to investigate some of the resources you have access to, and something you discover might be mind-blowing. It could be positive or negative, but it will result in clarity. It might take some time and research, but you're incredibly focused and willing to put in the effort.

Wednesday 21st

Responsibility is extremely important to you. For most of your life you've felt pressure to please and take care of everyone around you. Today you'll finally realise that you can take time of and retreat. You're just a human being, and it's vital that you recharge.

Thursday 22nd

The Sun is entering your area of possession, money and self-worth, thereby intensifying your focus on these matters. You should be wary of any contracts that don't have your, or your family's, best interests at heart. See if it's possible to cancel or adjust any agreements on your terms.

Friday 23rd

You may be tempted to spend a lot of money on new art equipment today, be that paint, brushes or a canvas. Make sure that your finances are in good shape first, and then try to stay within your budget. Whatever you buy, it doesn't need to be expensive to help you express yourself.

Saturday 24th

Another solution is knocking at your door. You might have found a new way to balance relaxing with working. This solution could manifest itself in your dreams or during meditation, so keep your notebook handy and take all hints seriously. Acknowledge how much power is inherent in retreating.

Sunday 25th

The Sun is embracing Mercury and imprinting your mind with a brand-new outlook on money. If you're used to lacking money, you'll now be able to see what's really and truly possible for you when have money, and even invest or create savings.

Monday 26th

You're focused on implementing your recent insights and discoveries into your everyday routines. The way you handle your money is changing, and you're likely to set up a housekeeping book, write a shopping list, or plan your budgets. This could be fun, and it'll help you to feel more in control.

Tuesday 27th

Today asks for a little escape from reality. Create some time and space for daydreaming, reading a book, or seeing a movie. Allow a flair of magic to fill the air and hone in on your intuition. Put logic aside for a moment. You know life is all about balance.

Wednesday 28th

This is a powerhouse of a day. Mercury is retrograding back into Libra, so you might need to rethink and reinvestigate something about yourself. Venus is also joining Mercury, helping you to create the most beautiful persona. Emotionally, you are focusing on your relationships, but you cannot escape yourself.

Thursday 29th

Even though something may have felt off recently, you still want to connect and relate. Approach your partner or friend with loving compassion, and you might be able to get closer to solving the conflict. Enjoy any time you spend with those that are already in alignment with you.

Friday 30th

Small frictions may arise within your family, but don't make mountains out of molehills. Equanimity is a welcome trait, and it will help you to focus on the bright side of life. You might also be in for a sensual experience, like a delicious meal or massage.

Saturday 31st

Trick or treat, that's all you need. However, make sure you treat yourself before treating everyone else. Share your resources, but don't give everything away. Draw a line and be clear about your boundaries. A surprise may be coming your way, and it could be very exciting.

NOVEMBER

Sunday 1st

There are still some surprises to come regarding your finances, but Jupiter will be able to help. In this case, somebody from your family is taking Jupiter's role so you have nothing to fear. It might just be the very thing you need for greater clarity, and to push through with your new mindset.

Monday 2nd

Solid foundations always prove themselves to be valuable. Based on today's foundation, you have the opportunity to open many new doors. The difficulty will be making a choice. Each and every one is tempting, but which allows you to broaden your mind and beliefs while still being of service?

Tuesday 3rd

Another question about your future choices presents itself today: what will your partner say? It would never be your preference to set out on a new journey alone, so you should aim for something you can do together. The chances are you'll find something that's a great fit for both of you.

Wednesday 4th

Congratulations on the hard look you recently took at your finances and resources. You've done enough rethinking and planning, so Mercury can now move direct. With the Moon in its current position, you'll feel ready to integrate and implement everything, and can set sail towards the future.

Thursday 5th

You'll be asked to be your own best friend today. You offer so much help and support to everyone else, but are you forgetting someone? If you can comfort yourself, it will make all your relationships easier. This will also help you to release some of your high expectations and allow you to feel happy within.

Friday 6th

Make self-love a new priority. You can practise it right away and will see the effect it has on the tension that's lingering within your vocation, home or relationship. If you're in alignment, you can balance it out easily. You must value yourself in order to become a master of equilibrium.

Saturday 7th

The weekend's here just in time, and you'll want to be out with your best friends. A shopping trip might be what you have in mind, with one or two stops for coffee and a tasty lunch. You may invest in something that emphasises your amenities.

Sunday 8th

Today, you might be forced into competing with your friends. Who has the most beautiful home? Who drives the latest car? Who goes on the best holidays? This will sit uncomfortably with you. Try to remind everyone gently that money cannot buy the most essential things in life.

Monday 9th

All your master skills are needed today because Venus and Mars are in opposition. Both are strong, but you have the advantage of knowing that compromise is necessary. Let love be the only rule and use your diplomatic skills to guide the negotiations. Love always wins!

Tuesday 10th

You could feel edgy throughout the day as you're coming
to terms with what you discovered about your new persona.
Maybe you're surprised about the potential you unearthed
from within. Pat yourself on the back. You did a great job,
and there's even more to come.

Wednesday 11th

You may enjoy a little retreat from the world today and
will find some grounding by walking through the autumn
landscape. Like the trees, let go of the leaves and create space
for the new to arrive in your life. The cup has to be emptied in
order to be filled.

Thursday 12th

Take a look in the mirror today. Not the usual look to see if
your hair's okay; look deep into your eyes and appreciate your
uniqueness and beauty. If you cannot see it, look again and
remember that real beauty doesn't conform to ideals. It radiates
from within.

Friday 13th

It's the third and final act of Jupiter conjunct with Pluto. This
time, Saturn takes a look across his shoulder to make sure
they're behaving themselves. You've been through an intense
transformation, and this is the final stroke to make sure
it's the best it can be for you. You should have a stable and
optimistic outlook.

Saturday 14th

There are no coincidences in the universe. Mars is finally moving direct in your relationship sector, which means there's finalisation with the re-evaluation and adjustments in your relationships. At its best, this situation has taught you some new ways to act, and you can now look forward to enjoying improved connections.

Sunday 15th

Today's New Moon in Scorpio is perfect for setting a new financial goal. This could be saving a specific amount of money, earning more or even becoming financially free. Set your intention and maybe plant a seed, together with some coins. Alternatively, plant a money tree.

Monday 16th

Venus and Jupiter are locked in a dispute, which may leave you unable to see the blessings within your current situation. Even when something is challenging, there's always a gift inherent in every obstacle you overcome. What can you learn from this situation? Where can you grow?

Tuesday 17th

There might be some unexpected costs related to your neighbourhood or siblings today. See if you can find an answer within the family, as this will be the smoothest solution. Remember, you don't need to carry the burden on your own, especially if it isn't even your burden.

Wednesday 18th

Some minor conflicts are coming up, but they aren't worth investing your energy in. Don't pull the trigger, and don't be triggered yourself. Otherwise, you may say something that causes embarrassment. If you do, shrug your shoulders and laugh it off. This is often the easiest way to dissolve tension.

Thursday 19th

If you're thinking about signing a new contract regarding money or savings, make sure you talk it through thoroughly with your family first and examine the small print carefully. You should all be in agreement about what you are signing in order to avoid conflict and tension in the future.

Friday 20th

Your urge for liberation and self-expression is huge today, but you may feel inhibited. It's possible that you need something extraordinary but cannot afford it at the moment. You might be tempted to spend the day sulking, but it would be wiser to find a creative solution instead.

Saturday 21st

The energy shifts dramatically today. With Venus entering your area of money, possessions and finances, your funds may receive a boost. Elsewhere, the Sun is entering Sagittarius, so a short journey could be on the horizon. You should also expect more messages, phone calls and meetings than usual.

Sunday 22nd

You are about to enter a very busy time, so you should reserve today for yourself if possible. You can use it either to reflect, create a plan or to retreat from everything. A mixture of all three could be viable too. By now, you should be able to recognise the importance of stepping back.

Monday 23rd

You might want to check and clean your possessions today. What's still useful, what's still to your taste and who might like it if you no longer want it? Some things could be gratefully received within your family, so you don't need to worry about having wasted your money.

Tuesday 24th

Create time for togetherness today, if you can. Do nothing except enjoy each other's company and dream away to the land of the unknown, of possibilities and colourful adventures. You could also watch a classic movie at home or go to the theatre, if you prefer.

Wednesday 25th

As with yesterday, you still want to spend lots of time with your partner or meet with your best friends. It's almost December, so you might want to go on an early visit to a Christmas market where you can immerse yourself in the festivities. Let the joy of the season start to soak into you and lift your spirits. It's the time of year to be with those you love.

Thursday 26th

Nobody's allowed to stand between you and your family. If someone's in conflict with your loved ones, then they're in conflict with you. Use your diplomatic skills and leave all judgements to one side. Respond and don't react. You know the difference.

Friday 27th

You'll need some excellent grounding to stay calm today. There could be a dispute about money, specifically if it's all yours or if taxes or fees have to be paid. It's highly possible that fees are indeed due, but they should be affordable. You will be better prepared next time. Perhaps starting a budget spreadsheet or finding a new app to help will make this easier to plan for.

Saturday 28th

You have made many beneficial adjustments to your budget this year, and you may discover today that you have more money at your disposal than you realised, which is a relief after yesterday's concerns. You could use these surplus funds to treat yourself, but it might be wiser to invest them. Let your money work for you.

Sunday 29th

This is a Sunday to enjoy family and home life. You can easily create a cosy and comfortable atmosphere, and some quality food will add to it. In the evening, your focus may shift to questions about your future, and what it may hold for you. Watch your dreams.

Monday 30th

Today's Full Moon in Gemini is also a partial lunar eclipse, and you might be able to see it in the sky if you're lucky and an early riser. This Full Moon is about your attempts to create a free, colourful and beautiful future. What have you set up so far? Do you like it?

DECEMBER

Tuesday 1st

Today may feel as if the Sun is rising higher and shining brighter than it did before. This is likely because Mercury is entering Sagittarius, bringing an emphasis on hope, faith and optimism. For you, that will mean being emotionally in tune with your goals and future.

Wednesday 2nd

Regarding your vocation, you might want to organise a special event or set up a charity for animals or humans that need shelter. It's your sincere desire to make this a fantastic festive season for everyone, and you'll have the energy and drive to do so.

Thursday 3rd

Someone might be trying to prevent or discourage you from realising one of your pet projects. Whatever their motive is, don't allow them to succeed. Asking for their help might just be the best way to disarm their destructive intentions, and their ideas may actually improve your project.

Friday 4th

Today, you may need to win the approval of authority figures. It's most likely that you cannot move forwards with your plans without their permission, so make sure your plea appeals to them. The promise of improved status or public attention might be the key to getting their compliance.

Saturday 5th

It's time to shine, and you can count on your partner's support, as well as the support of your colleagues. Now you need to dare to show full integrity and go for your cause. You'll likely receive positive feedback from the community, and possibly even achieve more than you expected to.

Sunday 6th

You'll probably want to spend the day keeping busy and connecting to as many people as possible. In the evening, make sure you have some time just for yourself to recharge and process all that's happened throughout the last week. There's still much more to come.

Monday 7th

Your mood is more introverted and reflective than of late. Helpfully, you might unexpectedly get an extra day off. Don't ask any questions, just be grateful and make good use of this day. This will probably mean making plans, as well as thinking problems through. Try to incorporate some meditation into your day too.

Tuesday 8th

Today is great for rolling up your sleeves and tackling household chores. That may sound like a lot of hard work, but it will suit your mood perfectly. The only potential hindrance will be if anyone else is home at the same time. If so, encourage them to go out and leave you to it.

Wednesday 9th

One of your expectations may not be met today. As you know, these are sometimes too hard for others to realise. Not everyone is capable of doing what you can do, so try not to show your disappointment. Instead, use the opportunity to explore, and release, any other unrealistic hopes you may have. You will feel lighter for it.

Thursday 10th

You may feel grumpy or disappointed today. Instead of drowning yourself in pity, see this as the perfect opportunity to broaden your mind and your beliefs. People are different. They have different values and make their own choices. Try to understand their viewpoints or merely ask and listen. Variety makes the world richer.

Friday 11th

It's the perfect opportunity to throw some old beliefs out of the window. If you're able to, you will create a chance to relate to people on a whole new level, which is precisely what you want. Write these limiting ideas down, freeze them or shred them. Once you have let them go you will have room for new possibilities.

Saturday 12th

It's a beautiful day for a beautiful day. Your relationships are much improved, and you may also have some extra money. What do you want to spend it on? Make sure you invest in something for yourself and don't spend everything on Christmas presents. Time is a valuable investment too.

Sunday 13th

Make it a slow Sunday, but not a lonely one. You'll likely either be on the phone for most of the day or receiving visitors. You will be able to share lots of lively conversations and stories. Find a moment of stillness, perhaps by sitting by candlelight in the evening, to maintain balance.

Monday 14th

Today's New Moon in Sagittarius places an emphasis on finding new ways to believe, affirm and communicate. You may decide to interact with new people or in a new language and will have all the resources needed – including the wisdom and knowledge. There's no reason to hesitate.

Tuesday 15th

With Venus entering your area of communication and short-distance travel, you'll find much value when exploring this area. This is an excellent time to go on a trip or to plan and book one. Your partner feels exactly the same as you and will support your efforts.

Wednesday 16th

With so much excitement in the air, make sure you have some healthy foods in the house to support your immune system. Stress could easily affect your wellbeing, but you can prevent issues by taking good care of yourself. Find the balance between indulgence and restraint.

Thursday 17th

Saturn is leaving Capricorn, and his entry into Aquarius opens up awesome possibilities for you. These should help you live your life with more fun, joy and passion, whilst renewing the ways in which you express yourself.

Friday 18th

Mercury embraces the Sun today. After the recent powerful New Moon, this is like the next step in developing new ways to communicate. It will help you to relate to the people you know, as well as to those you have considered strangers so far. Allow some days to achieve clarity, and enjoy the new things you are discovering.

Saturday 19th

Jupiter is about to leave Capricorn. Much work has been done in expanding your family structures and your sense of responsibility. If all went well, you are now left with a more positive attitude and a new sense of freedom within your existing structures. Welcome to the next adventure.

Sunday 20th

Jupiter is more than happy to dive into quirky Aquarius where he can expand your sense of self-expression. Just as he enters, he encounters Saturn. This meeting is beneficial, as it will help you to set boundaries and prevent you from overdoing anything. Enjoy the ride, and the new sense of freedom you have from establishing healthy boundaries and space for yourself.

Monday 21st

You might be keen to celebrate the winter solstice today, and with this the Sun enters your area of home and family. It's the first time in three years that the Sun has been here without Saturn, and it will feel as though a weight has been lifted off your shoulders.

Tuesday 22nd

There is just one thing you need to consider today: which family to celebrate Christmas with? Yours or your partner's? A possible solution would be to invite them all to your home. If so, you'll likely be very busy during the next few days. If you have already planned this, make sure you've made time for yourself in the days ahead. Don't exhaust yourself trying to make everyone else happy.

Wednesday 23rd

Do you really want to have a power struggle just a few days before Christmas? Save your energy and time and focus on love instead. Make sure everything's set up as fairly as possible. If anyone complains, try not to pass judgement. See if you can find a better solution, but remember you can't always please everyone. Try to be as fair as possible, including to yourself.

Thursday 24th

Christmas Eve is here. As a smart Libran, you may well have lightened your load by asking family or friends to help out on the prep work for tomorrow's celebrations. Take a breath today and ignore anything that isn't perfect. Christmas is about love, not perfection. Take a breath to appreciate the good things surrounding you today.

Friday 25th

Enjoy today, and all the surprises that may well be in store for you. There could be unexpected guests, food and, undoubtedly, presents. Overall, the energy is positive and optimistic. You'll have the most comfortable time if you go with the flow, and don't feel the need to control everything. Happy Christmas!

Saturday 26th

You'll be asked to forget your chores and let the magic of Christmas take over today. Realistically, that may not be possible. However, you could balance both if you ask for your family's help. Tackle your to-do list early on in the day, and then enjoy time together later on.

Sunday 27th

As the new year celebrations approach, the Moon enters your area of travel, vision and exploration. It might be hard for you to sit down and relax, as you feel an excitement rising within. Channel the energy into something practical but fun, such as researching potential holiday destinations for 2021.

Monday 28th

An unexpected opportunity could knock on your door today, and it could literally be the ticket to your future. Whatever shape or form this may take, be sure not to turn it down. It's not usually in your nature to be daring, but you'll be conquering new frontiers either way.

Tuesday 29th

Happy Full Moon in Cancer! It's time to look at all you've achieved by following your vocation this year. Achieved is not actually the right word. Shared, given or nurtured would perhaps be more appropriate. Let your heart fill with gratitude and pride.

Wednesday 30th

Your current surroundings might not be the right setting
to get in contact with new people or practise new ways of
communication. You need to get out and connect somewhere
else. It's also likely that following your vocation will offer some
practical opportunities for learning.

Thursday 31st

It's New Year's Eve once more. This year has been intense,
and it has brought lots of changes and shifts. Thankfully, 2021
will offer you a lighter experience. The key for you is to find
balance in everything you do, and to value yourself as much as
you value others.

Libra

DAILY FORECASTS
for 2021

JANUARY

. . . .

Friday 1st

Happy New Year and welcome to 2021. The year begins on the back of a Full Moon in your career sector. You may have seen the culmination of a work project or perhaps you had an end of year deadline and this has now been achieved. Look forward to your rewards.

Saturday 2nd

You may have some loose ends to tie up regarding your most important relationships this week. A final push is needed to get a joint project off the ground. If this is a love affair use your tact and diplomacy whilst keeping the momentum going. Don't let it exhaust you too much.

Sunday 3rd

The Moon is in your hidden sector. You may want to be alone and process some thoughts. It's possible that you're already in work mode and need time and space to get everything in order before returning for a new year. Get out the planners and diaries and schedule time for yourself too.

Monday 4th

Today you may have to balance your mundane duties with your private time. You may be called upon to be of service to a group or have an urge to follow your spiritual calling. This may conflict with your need to get organised and free up some time for yourself.

Tuesday 5th

This morning the Moon shifts into your sign. You may feel this as a return to normality and routine. Mercury meets Pluto today in your family sector. Listen carefully as they are discussing a new mission regarding how you take care of your tribe. Duty and responsibility will be the themes.

Wednesday 6th

Mars spends his final day in your relationship sector. This can be a highly active time and you may experience this as arguments with a lover, or exhaustion. Perhaps you have done all you can to meet someone halfway and now is the make or break period. Stay calm and centred.

Thursday 7th

Mars moves into your intimacy sector. He'll add some fire to your normally sensual intimate life. If a love relationship has changed, expect Mars to take you to places you may have never visited before. Sex, food, money and beauty will be high on the agenda with Mars here.

Friday 8th

Today you may notice that things get intense. You may be secretive about what you hold dear. You will need to assess where you feel vulnerable and how much you're willing to share right now. Your possessions can become obsessions so be careful to place value on the right stuff.

Saturday 9th

Mercury enters your creative sector today. You'll be very outspoken now in love, art and self-expression. Venus also shifts signs into your family sector where she, as your ruler will bring more harmony and love to a sometimes too strict environment. Split time between family and lovers equally today.

Sunday 10th

Mercury meets Saturn in your family sector. You can expect a lot of chatting, gossip or family banter. You must be careful not to overstep boundaries today. Mercury wants you to laugh and have fun, but Saturn may lay the law down and remind you what's acceptable.

Monday 11th

Speedy Mercury now meets Jupiter. This is a more light-hearted connection as Jupiter wants you to have joy and optimism. Perhaps there's an elder family member you didn't manage to meet up with over the holidays. Much laughter can be had when these planets meet, use this energy well.

Tuesday 12th

The Moon sits in your family sector and you may have more of a sense of duty and responsibility now. Family comes first and there may be a fear of outsiders. Be careful of what you say today as there's a chance that a secret is spilled and upsets someone.

Wednesday 13th

A New Moon occurs in your family sector today. This is a chance to set intentions and more resolutions regarding your tribe. You may find that there's obstructive energy that's preventing you from enjoying a midweek treat or time with a lover. This will irritate you.

Thursday 14th

The energy today is quite tough to navigate. You wish to say what's on your mind, but this will upset the balance and ultimately you. This will trigger an explosion of some kind and you may find that you are back-pedalling and making amends. Say centred and calm.

Friday 15th

Yesterday's energy may still be lingering. The Moon is in your creative sector and there's a chance that you find a new way of expressing yourself and keeping the peace. You are mindful of other's feelings and careful that you don't upset them. This is clever and responsible.

Saturday 16th

You have the opportunity to make this weekend a time when you merge your duties and own personal quests. You can be idealistic and ignore the hard facts but somehow this works to your advantage. Don't take the world on your shoulders, offer your experience and wise guidance instead.

Sunday 17th

Jupiter's squaring off with Uranus today. It's likely that you witness a larger than necessary disruption to your intimate life. Alternatively, this energy can provide you with a massive breakthrough or change of tack that you hadn't considered before. Take some time to look at things from another perspective.

Monday 18th

This morning the Moon moves into your relationship sector. You may be fired up with ideas or dragged along with another and their goals and aspirations. This could be tiresome unless you find a way to keep it balanced and joyful. What's in it for you?

Tuesday 19th

The Sun shifts into your creative sector. You'll notice that your self-expression will be more heartfelt now. This is your chance to shine. Experiment with new projects in art, poetry or love. You may also find that you attach yourself to a worthy cause now and this inspires you to connect with others.

Wednesday 20th

Mars and Uranus meet today. Together they're highly volatile so be warned. As they're in your intimacy sector you may find that this takes a special relationship up many levels. It may also bring aggression and instability. Try to use this energy in a positive way.

Thursday 21st

The Moon now meets Mars and Uranus. However this energy has manifested for you, you will now be so emotionally involved that it affects you deeply. There may be a feeling of boundless energy and restrictions at the same time. Stop, get centred and breathe. This will pass soon.

Friday 22nd

Today is a good day to enjoy some luxury with a partner. If there's making up to do, then a good meal or other sensual experience will work wonders. You may now see that something has ended and made space for new things to enter your life. What will you explore next?

Saturday 23rd

As the Moon moves into your travel sector, you find that you're in two minds about places you would like to visit. You like it hot then cold, you desire to visit a city then decide on a beach. These are questions you don't need to decide on straight away.

Sunday 24th

The future draws you away to distant lands. Do some research with a travel documentary or look at higher education to see what really attracts you. Today, as the Sun meets Saturn in your creative sector, you wonder just how far you're prepared to go.

Monday 25th

You may be conflicted today as your drive and energy are not syncing with your desire to see more of the world. Why not get creative about this and look at your wider friendship or interest groups for inspiration? This evening you find comfort in your work and status.

Tuesday 26th

The Moon is in your sensitive career sector. It's likely that you're a parent figure at work and must listen to everyone's problems. This is commendable as you're noticed for your ability to create a safety zone and keep healthy boundaries. Remember to strengthen your own too.

Wednesday 27th

The Moon's opposition to your ruler and Pluto means that today you may be subtly manipulated. Be protective, not defensive. Try not to be duped into being a scapegoat or taking the brunt of the work. Take a stand and exercise your skills of mediation if you must.

Thursday 28th

Today there's a Full Moon in your social sector. What has come to fruition for you over the last six months? It's possible that you see conflict with many different people now and you must take a side. Your ruler Venus sits with Pluto and asks that you let something go.

Friday 29th

The Sun meets Jupiter today in your creative sector. This is
a perfect opportunity to get out your soapbox and make sure
that you're seen, heard and witnessed. However, this may also
make you belligerent and express bullying behaviour. Use this
energy positively, no-one likes a show-off.

Saturday 30th

Tomorrow, Mercury will turn retrograde in your creative sector.
Use today to back up all your devices and double-check all travel
plans. Don't sign a new contract or start a new project now as it
will fall to the wayside and fail. Take time to be alone with your
thoughts today.

Sunday 31st

Mercury retrograde begins. In your private life, you may be
looking at something from a different perspective. Consider
the difference between surrender and sacrifice and ensure
that you're not being taken for granted in your everyday
duties. You have the energy to move a mountain today.

FEBRUARY

. . . .

Monday 1st

Venus enters your creative sector today. As your ruler, she
will pay special attention to bringing beauty to your artistic
endeavours. You may also earn money from this as Venus loves
her little luxuries. Network with others for new possibilities,
but try not to only see people as opportunities.

Tuesday 2nd

This is a particularly fortunate day if you can curb your natural
instincts somewhat. The Moon is in your sign making you
emotionally balanced. You may have an idea of what you wish
to create and express now. This could be words of love or
something for the collective to enjoy.

Wednesday 3rd

This afternoon you may see jealousy creeping in, and this
will throw you off balance. Your home and possessions may
require an overhaul. Don't be too hasty or impulsive if you're
decluttering as you may regret it later. Check your bank
balance as you may have funds available to treat yourself.

Thursday 4th

Today is rather intense and you may struggle to reconcile your
basic instincts with good old-fashioned courtesy. You may be at
a tipping point and ready to blow a fuse and this will upset you.
Do your best to look at another point of view.

Friday 5th

It's likely that you feel some effects from Mercury retrograde today. This may leave you with a bitter taste in your mouth and the inability to remedy the situation. If you can't control or harmonise this, try to make the best of it and find the lesson within. Look for the value and how it has affected your own self-worth.

Saturday 6th

Venus meets Saturn today. This combination will have you making or creating but playing by the rules. Saturn is a hard taskmaster and doesn't like it if you go beyond a comfort zone or get too extravagant. Of course, Venus wants the opposite. Be good and find the balance.

Sunday 7th

Today you wish to connect with your dreams and visions. However, this won't be easy as there will be some confusion about what those truly are. You must look for your true north first. Venus agitates Uranus and causes some commotion in your intimate relationships. This might be a good thing.

Monday 8th

With the Moon now in your family sector you are duty-bound to be responsible and concentrate on home affairs. Mercury has nothing to say to you today and your job is to listen. You may feel triggered by another's behaviour and take the high road.

Tuesday 9th

The Moon meets Pluto and you may feel in control of your emotions. This satisfies you as you don't like being out of kilter. It's possible that you need to be the responsible one in the family and people look to you to maintain the status quo. This isn't always easy.

Wednesday 10th

This is a day of swiftly changing emotions. Your desire to speak from the heart may be frowned upon by some and encouraged by others. If you're unsure what to do, pause and before you speak ask yourself if it is kind, true and helpful.

Thursday 11th

The Moon meets Mercury today and you could be having a heart and head battle which doesn't go down too well. A New Moon in your creative sector may help to stabilise you as you now have an opportunity to set goals and intentions regarding your art, love and self-expression.

Friday 12th

Following on from yesterday, your mind and emotions are easier to deal with. Venus and Jupiter have combined to give you a boost of joy and harmony. You have a smile on your face as you go about your mundane duties and connect to others. A happy surprise may come your way.

Saturday 13th

Today you gain some insight into your true north. Spend some time listening and receiving wisdom from others before making up your mind. Take everything in and weigh it all up. Your path is yours alone and only you can walk it. Do you have the energy for it?

Sunday 14th

Merging and connecting with wise people fills your spiritual needs today. However, be careful that you don't get misled or beguiled by false teachers. The truth is out there but with Mercury retrograde meeting expansive Jupiter, there's a possibility that you are led astray.

Monday 15th

Relationships, especially the close intimate ones, may be on a roller-coaster today. The Moon sits in this sector and connects to Saturn and Jupiter in turn. This restrictive then expansive energy may make you a little dizzy. Let it pass. Don't act on any particular feelings just yet.

Tuesday 16th

An outgoing Moon now gives you a little bit of peace and pleasure. You may find that love relationships get a boost of harmony. The only downfall of this is that you feel that you lose yourself and wish to stay in control. Relax, enjoy going with the flow for once.

Wednesday 17th

This is a tricky day and can cause you some grief if you try too hard to find reason and logic. The Moon enters your sensual intimacy sector and instantly bumps into Uranus, the disruptor. You may have an awakening of some kind but feel guilty about it afterwards.

Thursday 18th

The Sun now warms up your sector of health and mundane duties. You will go about your chores with a light-hearted spirit and be eager to be of service to others. Stay on track and don't let others take you for granted. Your drive and energy get a boost today.

Friday 19th

The celestial lovers, Venus and Mars are squaring off. You may see some conflict within your intimate relationships. Venus wants to share the love, but Mars wants it kept private and very much to himself. How might you harmonise this situation? It may be better to hide away today.

Saturday 20th

As the Moon hits your travel sector you find that you're reaching out and wishing to expand your boundaries. What more is out there for you? You could mull this question over and over and still not get any closer to the answer until you make the first step.

Sunday 21st

Mercury goes direct today and will retrace his steps from the last three weeks. You may get a déjà vu experience and with hindsight, you can do something a better way. Look at what triggers you and how you can move forward in life. Follow your heart now.

Monday 22nd

As the Moon drops into your career sector you may find
that your parenting instincts come out and you're fiercely
protective over your work colleagues. Here is where you stand
up for the underdog and take care of the weak or new. This is a
strength which is not unnoticed.

Tuesday 23rd

Water energy makes you emotional and sympathetic. You are
sensitive to those around you and can use empathy to feel as
they do. Your Libran skills of mediation and seeing both sides
will help you today as you steer others in the right direction.
Well done.

Wednesday 24th

Your energy picks up and you pass this onto those around you.
There may be a trigger from your home sector which niggles
you and needs you to be strict and hard. This will be difficult to
navigate as you're more inclined to be soft and intuitive today.

Thursday 25th

The Moon dips into your social sector but you don't feel much
like getting involved with groups today. There's a muddle of
different energies confusing you so it's best not to act. Venus
swims into your health and duties sector to teach you how to
look after yourself and get spiritual.

Friday 26th

The Moon drops into your hidden sector and opposes Venus today. You must look at what you do for others and what they do for you. Is it balanced? Is there equality? You may find that some activities get dropped or lovingly released because of differences now.

Saturday 27th

A Full Moon in your hidden sector will throw a spotlight on some dark corners of your psyche which need a tidy up. Your deepest parts may be filed and systematic but will still periodically need a clear out. What is it that needs to be brought up and healed now?

Sunday 28th

Strong earth energy keeps you grounded today. Your emotions, drive and self-control are all in sync and you're a solid dependable friend to someone important. They will see you as their rock or saviour. Be there for them but ensure that they don't become a psychic vampire to you.

MARCH

· · · · · · · · · · · · · · · · · ·

Monday 1st

What a great day for you to connect with and share your authentic self. Mercury will lend you the gift of the gab, Saturn will keep you respectful and responsible and Jupiter will make you happy and optimistic. This is an important day to be yourself and be appreciated for it.

Tuesday 2nd

Keep being you today. You're perfectly balanced in mind and emotions and this pleases you more than anyone else. If you have nothing pressing to do, take a step out of your routine and experience something new. You're perceived as a person that everyone needs in their life right now.

Wednesday 3rd

The Moon drops into your finances and values sector. You may find that this is the best time to check your bank balance or transform something around you. Bring a bit of seductive beauty into your home environment. This may shock some but will bring you satisfaction.

Thursday 4th

Today may be a little difficult as you may have to justify to others in your wider circle how you feel about certain things. Others may just not get you today. If you're true to yourself and your belief system, roll with it, they will have to come to terms with it.

Friday 5th

Mercury comes back to meet expansive Jupiter in your creative sector. You may find that there is a lot to talk about today. As the Moon is involved, this may mean that what you speak about is very close to your heart. Be respectful to those who disagree with you.

Saturday 6th

It's likely that you'll have a lot of running around to do today. You may be catching up with people or simply replying to messages and making nearby visits. Your self-expression is boundless so be careful as you may come across as a big head.

Sunday 7th

Family duties bring you home today and there may be some nice surprises in store for you. Venus helps you to connect to others and bring harmony to your tribe. You may see some spiritual value in serving others and this will be noted. You will be an example to those around you.

Monday 8th

Family life need not be so strict today. You're open to seeing other points of view and can express your dreams and wishes for the future. This is an easy-going day with calm energy so use it well. Merging with your dearest family will bring them back into alignment.

Tuesday 9th

As the Moon meets Pluto you feel self-controlled. Pluto, however, likes to see change and transformation so consider how you can grow your family values. This afternoon you're expressive and wish others to feel the simple joy in being able to speak their truths as you do.

Wednesday 10th

The Sun meets Neptune today. If you've needed clarity recently, this is when you get it. Neptune's fogs are burned away, and you can clearly see a focus, a direction or a point of view that may have been hidden from you. Store that experience away until the time is right to use it.

Thursday 11th

The Moon meets Mercury today. Your heart and head are perfectly in sync. This is a good time to sort out your thoughts and speak from the heart. This evening you may be offered a new viewpoint which will cause you some grief to get to grips with.

Friday 12th

Something is stirring you up today. You may need to check in with your health as Uranus is involved. Although it's a helpful connection to your health sector, you may now get some valuable insight into a little problem you've been having.

Saturday 13th

Today a New Moon occurs in your health and duties sector. This can act as a starting point for anything you wish to begin regarding these issues. An exercise regime or a wholesome spiritual quest may satisfy. Neptune hosts the Moon and you're emotionally invested in this new start.

Sunday 14th

Venus and Neptune meet today. This energy is so beautiful and surreal that you may be washed away to a fantasy island. Keep one foot on the ground and enjoy this ride. It may be shared with a lover for an extra delicious other-worldly experience. Stay safe and go with the natural flow.

Monday 15th

The Moon in your relationship sector is outgoing and adventurous. Let yourself be guided by a lover or close friend today. You may experience high activity and be thrilled by it. See to it that you aren't aiming to control anything today as the energy ebbs and flows nicely.

Tuesday 16th

Mercury flies into your health and duties sector. He will aid you in doing all your chores with time to spare. In that free time, you must ensure that you take care of your health as Mercury may also cause you to burn out if you're not in good form.

Wednesday 17th

Today may be a test of endurance for you. The Moon enters your intimacy sector and meets Uranus. You may desire to fill your soul and stomach with sensuous food or experiences, but this may do you more harm than good. Watch out for digestive upsets now.

Thursday 18th

If you ever wanted to switch off and surround yourself with fantasy, then today is that day. Pluto allows you to loosen your strict self-control whilst Venus and Neptune fill your mind and body with good food and company. You may have found a spiritual path or become successful at meditation.

Friday 19th

As a contrast, your mind may be full of chatter today. You could be processing new things and wondering if you are brave enough to step out into the wider world and travel. You may find this difficult to reconcile. To disperse this tricky energy, try doing some physical exercise.

Saturday 20th

Today is the Spring Equinox and the day and night are equal lengths. This is a very good time for you to pause and reflect on the year so far. With the Sun in your opposite sign you may feel upside down but you will soon adjust.

Sunday 21st

Venus has followed the Sun into your relationship sector
now. Your ego is at odds with your emotional self and you
may struggle to stay rational today. Enjoy a slightly different
way to feel and you may surprise yourself by how much
you learn from the experience. No need to tip the balance,
find it elsewhere.

Monday 22nd

Today your natural parenting instinct to those in the
workplace kicks in. You may be overly emotional or sensitive,
but you remain empathic towards others. Talk a problem
through with someone. You may be the listener or the talker,
either way, it will work out for you.

Tuesday 23rd

It's possible that you feel that you're being manipulated or
used in some way today. This may be because your arms are
open to those in need but sometimes your good nature is
dismissed. You may be extra-sensitive to criticism at work.
This will pass soon.

Wednesday 24th

Your social sector and wider groups require your attention
today. You may have a lot to say in your interest groups as
there's a lively discussion going on. Be careful that it does not
get too extreme. Keep it simple and respectful at all times.
Abide by the rules.

Thursday 25th

The Sun and Venus are having a rendezvous in your opposite sign. You may experience this as a spotlight on your close relationships or a heating up of love and desire. In your wider groups, you may be tempted to blow your own trumpet. Don't, you will be seen as an agitator.

Friday 26th

Today Mars in your travel sector is urging you to get out and experience the wider world. Be brave, be assertive or simply watch some documentaries and whet your appetite for the unknown. Foreign philosophies or religions may be strangely attractive to you now. What have you got to lose?

Saturday 27th

Your emotions turn inwards and become a little messy. You need time to process new thoughts and concepts and file them away for easy access at a later date. Take a day to yourself and get back in touch with your inner workings. Re-align yourself with your true north.

Sunday 28th

The Moon drops into your sign and gives you a Full Moon. Where have you achieved balance and harmony in your life in the last six months? Is there anything tipping the balance? Now is the time to do something about it and lovingly let something go.

Monday 29th

When you have a mind to re-orientate everything around you, the universe supplies the right energy. Today you feel the push and pull of Jupiter and Saturn, and the assertiveness of Mars. A little tweaking helps you to re-calibrate ready for the next round of forward motion.

Tuesday 30th

This morning you enter into an intense period that will help you bring about an ending and new beginning. The Moon in your sector of values and finances helps you to see what is cluttering up your life and home. Be ruthless and discard anything that isn't useful or bringing you joy.

Wednesday 31st

You have a mind to be detective-like and research whatever will help you stick to your spiritual path. Jupiter connects but in a way that reminds you to seek the truth and only the truth. Beware of false gurus and leaders that can glamour you and lead you astray.

APRIL
. . . .

Thursday 1st
Your sense of duty helps you to get through a long, busy day.
Messages, visits and chores may seem endless, but you will
plough through them with ease. Ticking things off your list
will make you smile, as will catching up with people you
haven't seen in some time.

Friday 2nd
Today you may have the difficult task of laying down the
law in family matters. This may stir up emotions which can
make your temper boil so stay calm. Your words will be your
strength today as you need to guide someone and take the
upper hand.

Saturday 3rd
You have an unpleasant aftertaste churning around your
mind today. There may have been a confrontation which has
left you feeling jaded and hurt. Disharmony is something
that you, as a Libran, dislike very much. Don't fret too much
as this will pass soon.

Sunday 4th
The Moon is in your family sector and you're milling over
recent nasty events. You may be feeling that you didn't handle
things very well. Time will tell if your words were heeded. You
may be pleasantly surprised today. Be soft and remind people
that you love them.

Monday 5th

Finding compassion at the heart of a warrior soul suits your
need for balance and harmony today. As the Moon meets Pluto,
you can transform how you feel about recent confrontations.
This afternoon you may have a stern talk with yourself or a
close friend and lover. This helps.

Tuesday 6th

As the Moon shifts, you may feel more like connecting and
sharing a passion. This is aided by Venus and Mars making
a helpful connection in your relationship and travel sectors.
Reaching out will help to soothe an open wound. When you're
ready, find a new focus in the wider world.

Wednesday 7th

This is a much nicer day with soft aspects to it. You may be
drawn out of your dark mood and taken care of by someone
special. Jupiter meets the Moon and enhances your mood
so if you can switch it to a happy one, you can receive much
joy today.

Thursday 8th

Take some time to consider recent events and where the
triggers came from. You are prepared to merge with spirit
to seek answers and this will soothe your soul. It's possible
to get a breakthrough and look at a problem in an entirely
new way.

Friday 9th

As the Moon meets Neptune in your health and duties sector you find the time to be still and listen to your inner voice. It may be urging you into action that you aren't ready for. Change is coming so use this space for quiet contemplation now.

Saturday 10th

This is a great day to spend time in partnership with a close friend or lover. Let yourself be guided and relax. This can be an active day but in a way that lifts your spirits and brings you back in balance. Much love and healthy discussion can be had today.

Sunday 11th

If you are spending time with someone special, today will be good for a heart to heart discussion. You may wish to get things off your chest or simply engage in a lovely debate about future plans and goals. You aim to please, and this will be repaid in kind.

Monday 12th

A New Moon in your relationship sector gives you the go-ahead to set intentions for your relationships. Venus is involved and as your ruler, she can bless those intentions with the beauty and harmony you desire. However, Pluto, the planet of change, asks that you end something now too.

Tuesday 13th

You would be wise to let yourself enjoy a delicious treat today. Sensual things such as touch, food or exotic scents will let you feel the height and depth of your being. You need to be grounded and these will help. Get out of your head and back into your body.

Wednesday 14th

Venus is about to leave your relationship sector. She asks that you consider what being a spiritual warrior means to you. How have you acted with love but firmness in the last few weeks? It's also time for you to plant those seeds of intention and watch them grow.

Thursday 15th

Venus comes home to your intimacy sector. Watch how she will help you to tend to new plans, discoveries and exploration of the bigger mysteries of life. Money may come in while she's here, but you must first discard anything that is preventing your personal growth. Do some weeding now.

Friday 16th

Today you find that you are reaching out to the future and wishing to learn more of the world. You may be fired up by thoughts of travel or higher education but undecided which paths to explore. You may have too many options and need to discard ones which are unrealistic.

Saturday 17th

The energy today is very tricky, and you'll need to exercise your Libran mind and be discerning. The Moon meets Mars and you're active but restless. This will be exaggerated unless you do something intellectual or physical. There's no time for dreaming today.

Sunday 18th

The Moon shifts into your career sector where you feel sensitive and protective. Unlike yesterday, today you must pay attention to your feelings and notice what makes you feel safe and nurtured. This is a complete contrast to yesterday and may be difficult for you to manage. Look to others for guidance.

Monday 19th

Both the Sun and Mercury enter your intimacy sector. This is a great combination for throwing light on the darker side life and making intelligent enquiries. Rooting around in subjects which both attract and repel you will be a good project for you to experience now. Have fun with this.

Tuesday 20th

Stay within your safety zone today as you may have feelings of manipulation or passive aggression coming from your family sector. Watch what you say as there may be a tendency to be more outspoken than you would normally. Keep your darker thoughts to yourself today.

Wednesday 21st

Friends and social groups can be interesting today. There's a chance that you come across a new idea or concept and this fires you up. Lively debates or even arguments can arise but either way, you will learn something new. Be respectful to others and remember personal boundaries at all times.

Thursday 22nd

You may feel the need to withdraw and be alone with your thoughts. Taking the time to process new things and organising your feelings will be highly beneficial to you. Mars is about to leave your travel sector and asks if you're ready to take a plunge into the unknown.

Friday 23rd

All sorts of surprises await you today. The Moon in your hidden sector makes great connections for you to explore your inner workings. You may discover something startling about yourself, but this will be all good. Venus and Uranus together make fireworks you will be amazed by.

Saturday 24th

As you're busy researching and filing parts of your psyche, you may notice what needs to be transformed or discarded. Mercury has joined Uranus to give you even more of a jolt in your intimacy sector. You may hear something shocking. This evening the Moon drops into your sign.

Sunday 25th

You may feel that you're back in your body and ready to face the world today. You're able to express yourself responsibly and maintain healthy boundaries. Mercury and Venus meet up and you may notice that your love talk is touching new borders. Be careful as this may offend.

Monday 26th

Today you must take a good look at what you have around you that makes you feel safe and secure. The Moon in your finance and value sector asks that you evaluate your belongings and consider if material objects really bring you peace. Get ready to make changes here.

Tuesday 27th

A Full Moon in your finances and values sector shows you just how much you have accumulated over the last six months. This is your chance to have a complete clear-out. You may also wish to look at your bank balance and see what you can do to enhance it.

Wednesday 28th

Pluto, the planet of permanent change, turns retrograde in your family sector. This will now act as the catalyst for you to compost your old things and make something new from them. Right now, you have the mind to do so, but this will not always be easy.

Thursday 29th

You are more active today. You're able to begin your clear-out and you start by looking at what's cluttering up your. Old messages may cause some grief, but you can let them go with love and know that there's now space for something else.

Friday 30th

As the Sun meets Uranus in your intimacy sector, you may see sparks of energy or have a 'Eureka!' moment. A light bulb flashes on and something is now so clear in your mind that you wonder why you've never seen it before. You know exactly where your true north is now.

MAY

. . . .

Saturday 1st

The Sun and Uranus are still producing electricity and you may be experiencing this as sexual activity or shocks and arguments. Hidden secrets may be surfacing. There's a possibility of burnout with this combination so be sure to look after yourself.

Sunday 2nd

Family matters need your attention now. You may be called upon to settle something or use your influence to calm and harmonise the family unit. A level head is needed now, and you're just the person they need. Your tact and diplomacy will be much appreciated.

Monday 3rd

Getting creative or returning to a passion will be good for you today. You have restless energy that you need to disperse, and you turn to an old project for completion. Venus and Neptune bring you inspiration and beauty. Enjoy what you do and share it with others as they will be uplifted.

Tuesday 4th

Mercury enters your travel sector where he will have a grand time filling your head with thoughts of learning more about the world. Look for what excites you and follow that route. Mercury will provide signposts and cues for you to make great discoveries. Watch out for them.

Wednesday 5th

Your emotions are expansive, and you wish that you could make everyone feel the same as you do. There may be a lot going on in your head but remember to follow your heart too. Too much thinking may give you a headache so let yourself go with the flow.

Thursday 6th

Be still and listen to your inner voice. This is the time to be patient and receptive. Surrendering yourself to the laws of the universe will let you balance yourself naturally. However, if you choose to sacrifice yourself and do others' bidding, you will miss your calling.

Friday 7th

As the Moon shifts you are awakened to new energy. This may be in your important relationships as you enjoy activities with a special person. You may rely on them to lead you to new things and will be quite happy to comply. Get to know someone better today.

Saturday 8th

Venus and Jupiter are squaring off and this energy may mean that your self-expression causes you to be selfish and hurt another. Boastful behaviour or passive aggression may surface. Keep things low key and retreat if need be. You will not achieve much so don't waste your energy.

Sunday 9th

Venus is leaving your intimacy sector and going travelling. This is a fortunate placement for you as she can bring the balance you crave to an area of your life you're quite undecided about. Emotionally, you're pulled to make an intimate connection or explore the darker mysteries of life.

Monday 10th

The Moon has her monthly visit to Uranus. Emotions can be highly unstable. There is a positive aspect of this as it's in your intimacy sector. The earth may move for you if you get close to that special person in your life. Deep feelings of love may surface.

Tuesday 11th

A New Moon in your intimacy sector marks a new beginning or a deeper level of trust being established. You must tread carefully. You're not the only one who dislikes upsetting the balance. Respect personal boundaries at all times and keep your own healthy and strong.

Wednesday 12th

The Moon and Venus meet up and you may find that your emotions are in sync with your desires. You may get what you wish. Uranus is still rumbling deeply and now connects to Mars who goes after what Venus wants. Express your desires and they will be yours.

Thursday 13th

Your heart and head have a little talk today and check in with one another. It's sometimes difficult for you to feel and emote openly as you're a rational, logical person. Listen to what your heart says and don't make it difficult for yourself by trying to justify everything.

Friday 14th

Jupiter has entered your health and duties sector. If you've been needing a tonic or a pick-me-up, this is it. Your health niggles may subside while he's here. You'll also find that you go about your mundane duties with a smile. Spiritual quests are favoured now.

Saturday 15th

This is an easy-going day where your emotions seem to go with the ebb and flow of your activities like a little boat. You will be happy to serve others, be sensitive to their needs and receive the same back from them. A great day to connect and use your intuition.

Sunday 16th

Your personal energy is tied in with your feelings today. You may be emotionally attached to something you need to let go of. This is causing you to cling on all the tighter. Feminine wisdom will guide you to make this transition easy and teach you how to honour the loss.

Monday 17th

It's possible that you feel extra sensitive or protective. The Moon opposes Pluto, who's nagging you to make subtle but permanent changes. Look to your home and work environments as a little tweak may make a massive difference. Spend on a small treat for yourself.

Tuesday 18th

A fiery Moon in your social sector may mean that you're involved in a group cause where a collective voice is needed. You may show some leadership qualities and stand up for yours and the groups' rights. It's likely that you come up in opposition against authority figures.

Wednesday 19th

Today your intentions need to be witnessed within your interest groups. There may be a lot of messages, emails or calls to be made. Communication will be at an all-time high and plans for big get-togethers or parties may be made. You may need to monitor this.

Thursday 20th

There's only so much social activity you can take before you need to retreat and process it by yourself. The Moon drops into your hidden and private sector and you have the time to pause and reflect on your position. You may like the responsibility you've been given.

Friday 21st

The Sun is now warming up your travel sector just in time for you to do something with its powerful energy. Indecisions may now be settled. Neptune sits right opposite and his fogs have been burned away by the Sun. If you look carefully, your dreams and aspirations will be clearly visible.

Saturday 22nd

Stop trying to justify your excuses for not moving today. Sometimes your need for equilibrium is a hindrance and you should go with the flow more. The Moon is now in your own sign, but you could be trying too hard not to upset the status quo.

Sunday 23rd

Saturn turns retrograde in your creative sector. You may begin to feel restricted or blocked in your expression and artistic pursuits. Use this period to slow down and pull back in. A little introspection will do you good. You need to repair or maintain your personal boundaries.

Monday 24th

When the Moon enters your finance and values sector, you may feel Uranus pulling on your emotions. Maybe a secret has been revealed. This influence can also mean that you have overspent and are regretting it. Money matters today, check your bank balance is healthy or find a way to make it so.

Tuesday 25th

You may have intense feelings about your personal growth. Your determination isn't yet at a level you can depend on. It's possible that you're feeling defensive or refusing to co-operate. Saturn makes a connection to the Moon and asks that you pull back if you feel doubtful.

Wednesday 26th

A Full Moon in your communications sector throws a spotlight on how you've been dealing with learning, teaching and researching in the last six months. Have you put enough effort in? Are the results what you desired? How can you go above and beyond to find what you seek?

Thursday 27th

Venus and Mercury combine to cheer you on and coax you out of a dark corner today. You have dreams and visions waiting for you to activate them. You may not be ready as this will include making decisions that you don't have enough information on.

Friday 28th

The Moon shifts into your family sector and you may use this to side-track yourself from other issues. No matter, this will not do you any harm. This is one area of life where you feel you have some control, and this suits you. Merge and connect with your tribe today.

Saturday 29th

Mercury goes retrograde today so maybe it's just as well you haven't committed to any travel or education yet. This may be a difficult day for you so use it to rest. Lie low until the Moon passes and you're rejuvenated. Do all the necessary Mercury retrograde checks now.

Sunday 30th

The rest of the weekend is brighter and has lighter energy for you to access. This is much needed after a heavy week. A quiet art project may satisfy, as will connecting to your wider social groups. Love will be simple and sweet today; you deserve this.

Monday 31st

The Moon meets newly retrograde Saturn. You may be sensitive to criticism. If you're energised, there's a chance you might rebel and do your own thing regardless. It's likely that you get a kick-start from somewhere and start your motor running after your true north.

JUNE

. . . .

Tuesday 1st

Insight comes your way and you may wish to grab it with both hands. The Sun meets the point of fate in your travel sector and is telling you that higher education and distant lands beckon. Your creative expression knows no bounds today. Make the most of these influences.

Wednesday 2nd

Venus enters your career sector. Your sensitivity will be tempered with more compassion as you take on new roles in the workplace. You'll be more brilliant than usual in achieving harmony and protecting the rights of others. People will look to you for wisdom and guidance.

Thursday 3rd

Your dreams and visions return to ensure you're on the right track. You're emotionally invested in this. This may feel at odds with your duties in the workplace, but it will work out. Venus and Jupiter combine to make you extra empathic and sensitive with everyone you meet.

Friday 4th

Mercury is filling your minds with doubts today. Don't ignore them but try to feel into what's triggering them. This can be solved and brought back into alignment. This is just a nod making sure that you have all the facts in order to go ahead.

Saturday 5th

Today can be an active time with a partner or close friend. However, this can also mean that hot disputes are likely and control issues will surface. The planet of war is opposing the planet of permanent change. There may be a battle for dominance in the air, but this energy will soon disappear.

Sunday 6th

You're more inclined to hunker down and enjoy a good movie that has deep issues and themes. It would be even better if you shared this with a lover over a good meal. Taste buds and senses are waiting to be tantalised. You need a thrill.

Monday 7th

The Moon makes her monthly visit to Uranus. As always with this meeting, you could see sparks fly in the area of intimacy or shared ventures. Jealousy is possible here too. Saturn is involved and asks that you remain respectful and not overstep another's boundaries. Don't push too far.

Tuesday 8th

The extra energy and assertiveness you experienced yesterday may now be channelled into another, healthier avenue. You find more tolerance and acceptance to make a shared vision work. There's something that needed to change and that may have simply been an attitude or opinion.

Wednesday 9th

The Moon in your travel sector churns up your emotions and you may be yearning for something, a path that you've recently decided on. When the time is right to act, you'll know. You must be patient and fill your heart with research and enquiry so that you're fully informed.

Thursday 10th

There's a New Moon in your travel sector. This is your chance to set goals and intentions regarding finding your own path and truth. However, this Moon meets Mercury retrograde and you must not act yet. This is the time to gather your information and allies before setting off on your hero's journey.

Friday 11th

Listen carefully and watch out for signposts. Mercury is in the heart of the Sun receiving downloads and upgrades. There may be an auspicious message coming your way. Mars enters your fiery social sector and will get the party started. Prepare for high activity here.

Saturday 12th

The Moon meets Venus and together they ask that you take today to nurture yourself. Whatever you like doing or eating, do it now. This energy lets you make a blanket tent and eat as much ice cream as you like, without guilt. Feed your soul and revitalise yourself.

Sunday 13th

The Moon joins Mars in your social sector and opposes Pluto. You may find that something exciting has dragged you away from your comfort zone. If you want to join in then do so, but you'll be just as happy having more me time before the week starts again.

Monday 14th

You may have a fuzzy feeling in your brain today and be unable to concentrate. A sluggish start to the week is likely. This influence won't last long so don't worry too much. You may be restless and impatient with yourself as you dislike feeling out of sorts.

Tuesday 15th

Today may be difficult in the areas of intimacy and expression. Mercury retrograde attaches himself to this and you may see conversations getting muddled or misunderstood. Stay away from taboo or risqué subjects and keep disputes to a minimum. You may upset or shock someone you respect so be careful.

Wednesday 16th

Turning inwards and feeling sorry for yourself isn't the way to go. You may feel at a standstill again, forever trying to balance how you feel. Stay in that place and spend time in solitude. You may wish to assess where you've been and where you think you're going.

Thursday 17th

Your dreams seem like a distant fantasy today. You can use this time to take an objective standpoint and look at what information you're missing. Your thoughts may go deeper than usual but you may be using more intuition too. Be logical and rational and discard what doesn't fit.

Friday 18th

As the Moon drops into your sign you become more aware of your outward projection and how you're perceived by others. You quickly regain your sense of equilibrium. Pluto and Mars send you energy and self-control. You're ready to make an action plan. Try creating a vision board.

Saturday 19th

It's possible that you feel defensive today and need a little more nurturing. Blockages and obstacles appear to be insurmountable. Hold on to your centre and don't allow yourself to be pulled in a direction that feels unnatural to you. This feeling will be temporary. Stay strong.

Sunday 20th

If everything seems to be slowing down, this is a cue for you to do the same. Intense feelings about what you hold dear, including your own self-worth, may cause you some grief. If you must do something, let go of your low self-esteem today.

Monday 21st

Today is the Summer Solstice and the Sun moves into your career sector. The longest day begs to be filled with activity. You may not be feeling sociable, but a solo celebration will do just fine. Jupiter turns retrograde today and will help you return to neglected creative projects. Restless energy can be dispersed through art.

Tuesday 22nd

You have a moment of great peace today and your low mood jumps up a few notches. You may see a glimpse of your dreams once more and will figure out how to care for your own needs and wants. Mercury turns direct and will bring you more important facts.

Wednesday 23rd

Conversations, messages and phone calls may fill your day. You're more outgoing and sociable. You may see power struggles and control issues between men and women or home and work, but you're able to mediate and bring everyone involved back into balance. Try not to overload your brain today.

Thursday 24th

A Full Moon in your family sector shows you how far you've come over the last six months. What may have seemed like a mountain then, is now a molehill. You may have achieved a great step or up levelled your status. A promotion is likely now.

Friday 25th

Neptune turns retrograde. You may think that your dreams are slipping away again but they aren't. This is your chance to either surrender and go with the flow or look at things from a different perspective. You may meet new people now who make you think differently.

Saturday 26th

When the Moon meets Pluto today, it also opposes Venus. This can be tricky energy to manage as it may mean that your nurturing instincts will clash with your duties and responsibilities. Use this brief passing to exercise your Libran skills of mediation and find your balance once again.

Sunday 27th

Venus enters your social sector. She'll become somewhat of a party girl here and you may find that your need for fun with friends increases. An elder or wise person may inspire you to talk about new and interesting things. You may even join a good cause.

Monday 28th

Don't give all your energy out to other people. This is easier said than done. The Moon meets Jupiter, newly retrograde, and whatever your mood is, it will surely be exaggerated by this energy. Merging and connecting with like-minded people may stabilise you but be sure not to be taken for granted.

Tuesday 29th

Today your mood is more upbeat and romantic. The Sun in your career sector connects to the Moon and gives you a loving, caring attitude which draws people to you. Be discerning and don't let energy suckers drain your good spirits. This is a good day to balance emotions and ego.

Wednesday 30th

The Moon meets Neptune today and you may struggle to stay alert as you get lost in Neptune's mists. Keep one foot on the ground by doing something physical or checking in with your body. Neptune retrograde wants you to switch off safely. Meditation will do you good.

JULY

. . . .

Thursday 1st

As the weekend approaches, you're inclined to make plans with a partner or special friend. You may be eager to party or just enjoy good food and company. There may be some opposition and a struggle between your personal energy and a person in authority. This can be frustrating.

Friday 2nd

Gentle energy removes any obstructions and allows you to move forward with weekend plans and activities. This may be because you're now observing protocol and realising that some things have a natural up and down before they get going. Express your future plans to someone close today.

Saturday 3rd

This afternoon is great for making your plans solid. You may need to look at your routine and assess how much of that is dictated by others. Take things slowly today and plod on through all your chores. There will be time to play or wallow in luxury this evening.

Sunday 4th

You may need to run and hide today. Planetary conditions are very unstable. The Moon meets disruptive Uranus and makes poor connections to Venus and Mars. If you're not prepared to back up what you think and say, then say nothing at all. Arguments are very likely.

Monday 5th

There's time to dream and get back in balance today. You may regain control of a family matter and your sense of responsibility returns. This may be because you've validated another person's point of view and after much consideration, you stand down. Well done, you've achieved harmony.

Tuesday 6th

As the Moon comes back to your travel sector, you find that once again you're thinking of reaching out and expanding your world. This may not be easy as you're still undecided. You need to be absolutely certain of something in order to proceed. Gathering facts and not fantasies will help.

Wednesday 7th

Today you have a little more direction and determination to broaden your horizons. Your social groups can help here so ask for their experiences and take all the information on board. You may still feel obstructed as Venus opposes Saturn; use this influence to pause and reflect.

Thursday 8th

You have a busy mind and need to offload some of what's inside. Your enquiries may be satisfied by watching a documentary or researching a place of interest. This is a simple way of bringing the world to your doorstep and keeping your mind busy with distraction.

. . . .

Friday 9th

A sensitive Moon in your career sector can make you feel protective about your aspirations. Maybe now's not the right time to ask for advancement up that corporate ladder. Sometimes you're happy and safe where you are. Other times you desire to feed your soul with a little more acknowledgement.

Saturday 10th

The New Moon in your career sector is your chance to start something different in the workplace. Maybe you did ask for that promotion after all. How can you switch up your job description to make it more caring and nurturing for both you and your team workers?

Sunday 11th

If you can grab a last-minute weekend social with your groups, then do so. You're fiery and can be the centre of attention within your friendships. You are honoured for being your authentic self in these groups. Mercury now enters your career sector and will help with that New Moon intention.

Monday 12th

Today has super energy for lovers and friendships. The celestial lovers, Venus and Mars, are very close, and both visited by the Moon. Your drive and desire are in sync and anything is possible now. You may even shock yourself by doing something out of the ordinary today.

Tuesday 13th

Mars and Venus meet in your social sector. If you prepared for this yesterday, then today you'll reap the rewards. Go after what you want with loving compassion and the support of your wider friendship groups. Online friendships will benefit from this energy and can achieve much when working together.

Wednesday 14th

Today you can use your inner filing cabinet and sort through your mind and thought processes. You may find those old ways of thinking are no longer relevant. Mars and Venus are encouraging you to embody the spiritual warrior and be true to yourself. Be bold and express your innermost desires.

Thursday 15th

If your dreams and passions seem a long way off, it's because the Moon is entering your own sign and your need for realism kicks in. Powerful energy from the Sun shows you that your dreams are attainable but only if you're not led by ego.

Friday 16th

Today you're sensible and responsible. You may have to look at your creative projects or your desire to speak out. There's something you wish to say but you must do it with all due respect to the receiver. This may be a work colleague so tread carefully.

Saturday 17th

You may be feeling romantic and outgoing as the Moon is connecting to Venus and Mars again. Don't let this side-track you from a more important issue today. It's possible that you see power struggles regarding your leadership and parenting roles. Pull rank on those not conforming to standards.

Sunday 18th

Intense feelings surface and you may be angry with yourself today. Money issues will need your attention, especially those accounts you may share with another person. You may need to find a new way of dealing with issues that are deeply sensitive and difficult for you to broach without conflict.

Monday 19th

The Moon drops into your communications sector and you may find that you're extra busy doing small jobs, sending emails and contacting people. However, the Moon here gives you the fire you need to get through these chores, and you may even meet new and interesting people today.

Tuesday 20th

Mercury and Uranus connect to give you new skills or help to solve a long-standing problem. If something has been eluding you, there's a chance that you'll now get a breakthrough. Something hidden may now pop out and surprise you. You will wonder why you never saw it before.

Wednesday 21st

This is a great day for getting support and encouragement from your friendship groups. Both sexes may combine to come up with innovative ways of showing up and being witnessed. You may become involved in a rally or protest march for a good cause. This will excite you.

Thursday 22nd

Venus now leaves your social sector and will be floating around your deepest hidden sector. As your ruler, she will organise your thoughts and bring clarity. The Sun enters your friendship sector so prepare for some late summer fun and social activity. Things are about to get busy in this area.

Friday 23rd

Today you manage to do your duties to others with grace and control. Your way of looking at things may have been changed by a casual remark recently, but this is all good. Your Libran skills of being discerning and looking at all sides of a story are working well.

Saturday 24th

A bright Full Moon in your creative sector throws the spotlight on your newer artistic ventures. This can be children, self-expression, love or rebelliousness. Where might you have had the opportunity to think outside the box and come up with something new or radical? It may have paid off today.

Sunday 25th

Difficult energy today can mean that you come across situations where you feel manipulated or unable to express yourself. You may need to be a more sensitive listener as someone leans on you or needs to use you as a sounding board. You may resist this role.

Monday 26th

More conflict or tricky situations come up and this may cause you some inner turmoil and a sleepless night. The Moon meets Jupiter in your health and duties sector so any emotions you were already feeling will be larger. Venus wants you to switch off and spend time alone if possible.

Tuesday 27th

Today you have a choice. Surrender to going with the flow or let yourself be sacrificed and scapegoated. If you choose the former, your higher vision will lead you back to your inner compass and you'll feel balanced and aligned again. The latter will only make you scattered and unfocused.

Wednesday 28th

Jupiter retrogrades back into your creative sector. You must now look at the attitudes and beliefs you have regarding your self-expression. You may have followed a route that is now lost to you. Go back to a point where you can restore equilibrium and wait there for a while.

Thursday 29th

Mercury is in your social sector just in time for the end of summer get-togethers. Expect a high volume of communication now. Mars has also shifted signs and has joined Venus in your private sector. You'll be driven to sort out your private thoughts and get rid of old habits.

Friday 30th

You may be overdue some treats and luxury. Shopping for your favourite foods and making a date with a good friend could be a good plan for today. You wish to discuss intimate things with someone and put the world to rights. Dinner, wine and philosophising are on the agenda.

Saturday 31st

It's possible that you find yourself between a rock and a hard place. Be very careful what subjects you discuss with social groups as you may be a little rebellious now and upset someone. Pick a side and stay there, you can't balance this one.

AUGUST

....

Sunday 1st

As August begins, you may find that something disrupts
your inner sense of groundedness. It appears that you have
a lesson to learn today. Mercury is in the heart of the Sun
receiving new downloads and it's your job to listen to an
elder or wise person.

Monday 2nd

Today your ego is likewise rattled by authority figures. You
may find that you're going against the norm and upsetting a
few people. There's a chance that you get angry and consider
retaliating or rebelling. This will do you no favours. Find your
centre and breathe.

Tuesday 3rd

Today you have a better sense of direction as the Moon meets
the point of fate and reminds you of your yearnings to improve
yourself. This is aided by the Sun and Mercury in your social
sector. Friends and wider social groups can be of great service
to you now.

Wednesday 4th

If you reach out and network with others, you'll get more
support than you first think. You may have to learn that the
road to your true north has some bumps along it, and you
must absorb these with grace. These triggers will help you
grow. Enjoy the ride.

Thursday 5th

Today is much quieter but your energy is high. You may be asked to parent a younger person or to look at your own emotional needs and what makes you feel safe. You'll be driven enough to see this through as it will fire up your sense of freedom.

Friday 6th

If there are others who are shocked by your outspokenness today, then let them be. It's your job to be as authentic as possible. You may have revelations coming from your inner psyche and these now need to be healed or acted upon. Control issues may surface from work and home.

Saturday 7th

This morning you're feeling braver and you dare to make your views heard. They may be radical and can stir up feelings of imbalance which you won't like. Keeping them to yourself will make you feel worse, you're doing the right thing.

Sunday 8th

A New Moon in your social sector seems to confirm that speaking your mind and making yourself heard is the best thing you can do right now. You'll need to get over the feeling of causing imbalance as life is not always stable. Learn to go with the ebb and flow.

Monday 9th

The Moon meets Mercury today and you may have feelings of upset or regret about speaking out. This will pass soon as the Moon drops into your private sector. Jupiter is sitting opposite and watching how you manage your emotions. Be careful as he'll tend to exaggerate them.

Tuesday 10th

Mars hosts the Moon now and together they can make your emotions aggressive or assertive. How you play this is up to you. With Venus close by, you're reminded to always do the best for yourself as self-loathing is not a good look. Harmony must come from within you before sharing it.

Wednesday 11th

Be very careful about how you respond to groups. Your viewpoint is important and valued but today you may go a little too far and upset the status quo. You may be seen as an antagonist. Look to Venus to help you maintain your inner peace. Make changes if necessary.

Thursday 12th

Mercury now joins the other planets in your hidden sector. This is good news as he's the expert at rooting around in dark areas and finding the gold or pearls of wisdom. Venus and Pluto connect to show you what you need to transform or get rid of.

Friday 13th

You may feel more settled today as you understand this process of clearing out your stuck thought processes. The Moon in your sign makes helpful connections to your self-expression. However, there may be a tricky situation which you have to take care of regarding family. Take it slowly and use your mediation skills.

Saturday 14th

Today you may have intense feelings about money, possessions and your own self-worth. Mercury is finding pieces of your psyche which have issues with these. Fortunately, you have the energy to deal with them and recognise that this is a healing process. Good for you.

Sunday 15th

You may come across an incident or belief system that shocks and upsets your system today. You're holding fast to your inner compass but may notice a wobble that you have to deal with. A short, sharp shock will soon have you re-calibrated and back on track.

Monday 16th

This may be a busy day of running around and getting messages delivered. You may have a very long 'to do' list today. Take it easy as this energy may drain your batteries and you'll need recovery time later on. This is best done when your ruler Venus enters your own sign this evening.

Tuesday 17th

If you have spare energy, pour it into social engagements or catching up with friends you may have neglected recently. You may feel like you're swinging away from your personal mission statement, but some time spent with friends is harmless and enjoyable. They may even put you straight again.

Wednesday 18th

The Moon drops into your family sector today and here's where you must put on your adult hat and be responsible. This may irritate your sense of self but today you must put others first or lay the law down. There are rules to abide by for everyone to observe.

Thursday 19th

Disruptive Uranus turns retrograde in your intimacy sector. This can have the effect of forcing you to try something new or accept a radical point of view. Mercury and Mars meet up in your private sector, prepare for action as subconscious material surfaces from the depths.

Friday 20th

Is there someone around you who's acting as a guide or mentor to you? You would do well to listen to this person today as you may have a very important, though harsh lesson to hear. This will knock you from your balancing point for a short while.

Saturday 21st

The Moon squares off with newly retrograde Uranus. Your creative or romantic projects may get a bump of some kind. There's the chance of seeing something differently or being challenged to come up with something completely new and innovative. Will you rise to the challenge or run away?

Sunday 22nd

There's a Full Moon today in your creative sector. This may show you what Uranus was hinting at. Think about your achievements over the last six months in this area. What are you proud of? What has come to completion? Celebrate your successes and reward yourself.

Monday 23rd

The Sun is now in your hidden sector. This will act as a source of enlightenment and realisation regarding issues you have struggled with, kept quiet or have simply not been able to reconcile. You may feel somewhat exposed and vulnerable but know that this will help in the long run.

Tuesday 24th

Use today to merge and connect with your spiritual life. You may need to switch off and meditate or practise yoga. Your heart and head are not in agreement and you must try to centre yourself and come back to a good place. Get back in touch with your true north.

Wednesday 25th

Mercury is playing tricks today is sending messages to Neptune. You may find that as soon as you have peace, you start to worry again. An active Moon in your relationship sector wants you to share a worry with a special person or let them lead you into physical activity.

Thursday 26th

You may find that there's a conflict of interests between your love life and your family as both need your attention. You may desire to be taken away and let someone else be the adult but at the same time, your family issues require you to be the grown-up.

Friday 27th

Today is one of those days where the best thing you can do is to buy yourself something nice such as your favourite food and enjoy some good company. This may not please Saturn who wants you to be responsible with money but if you're wise it need not be expensive.

Saturday 28th

Prepare for a little bump as the Moon meets Uranus. This will not be unpleasant and may come as a nice surprise. Venus is involved here so it will certainly be something that you deserve. It may be something that revs up Mars in your private sector.

Sunday 29th

This is a really good day for sharing your deepest desires with someone you care for deeply. The Moon makes favourable connections to the planets in your private sector and also Neptune who holds your dreams and visions. Allow yourself to fantasise with a lover.

Monday 30th

Mercury is done in your hidden sector and now comes out into the light. He flies into your own sign and will help you express your desires and needs now. There's nothing wrong with having needs and wants and you may do something about asking for these whilst Mercury is here.

Tuesday 31st

You may get a crisis of conscience today as you feel that your own requirements are less important than others. It's possible that you have two trains of thought running at the moment and can't fix on one. If in doubt, do nothing and wait until this energy passes.

SEPTEMBER
. . . .

Wednesday 1st

Today you may feel sensitive and believe that all negative remarks are aimed at you. With Mercury in your own sign, you may be more outspoken but can also be argumentative and defensive. This will not last long. Breathe deeply and you'll soon be back in balance.

Thursday 2nd

You have more energy and positivity today, but it will all be directed at what needs to be done to get through the day. If you can detach from your private thoughts and opinions and be professional, all will be well. There is potential to be over-protective and act out.

Friday 3rd

Get ready for the weekend. Your mundane duties can be put aside or quickly done and allow you some free time to spend with friends. You may have a need to be with those who nurture you and support your dreams. Conflict between home and work is possible.

Saturday 4th

Your wider social groups can be of great benefit to you now. There's a chance that you're challenged and will need to accept that you may not be able to fully grasp a new concept. Listen to those who know better than you and take things in slowly.

Sunday 5th

You may be shining your light within your friendship groups and you feel uplifted. Your sense of self-worth is good and enables you to fully participate in group activities. It's likely that you are learning an important lesson about the wider world and its philosophies and religions.

Monday 6th

The Moon is in your hidden sector and you need time to process new information and to justify it to yourself. You will need to look at both sides as you usually do. Pluto helps you to transform some of your ideas about status and social standing. This might niggle your sense of self.

Tuesday 7th

A New Moon in your hidden sector asks that you stop and reflect before acting on anything new. You'll need to do a thorough clean-out of beliefs that no longer serve you. Look again at what Mercury found and promise yourself that you will clear out the debris.

Wednesday 8th

Saturn makes a helpful connection to the Moon in your own sign today. Although still retrograde in your creative sector, you are being given a moment to evaluate how far you've come and how far you're prepared to go to share your individuality within a wider group.

Thursday 9th

The Moon meets Mercury in your sign. This is a great day for reconciling your emotions with your thoughts. If there are discussions or conversations to be had today, you'll speak from your heart. Be mindful that what you say may not always be received well by others.

Friday 10th

Today the Moon passes over Venus in your sign and they have an intuitive talk. You must realise that you're very much allowed to be yourself in any situation you're in. The message here is that you must never compromise yourself. This is terribly important.

Saturday 11th

Venus and the Moon both move into your secretive finance and value sector. Venus will now up her game in teaching you self-worth. She may even add to your bank balance or let you spend it guilt-free. You will have to ignore those who may be shocked by your confidence today.

Sunday 12th

It's possible that you lock horns with someone in authority today. It may be someone from your wider interest groups. You're assertive and will not move from your perspective. Later in the day you may feel differently and wish to make amends to anyone you may have upset.

Monday 13th

Getting in touch with others or simply networking for your day job will be the most important focus of the day. There's no time for dreaming as this is simply one of those days where you have much to do. Working steadily will make the day fly by.

Tuesday 14th

The Sun sits opposite Neptune and burns away the fog that has been gathering around your true north. You can get a glimpse of a different perspective to consider. This is information to file away in your innermost thoughts and sort through at a later date. Duty calls you this afternoon.

Wednesday 15th

Mars now enters your sign. This heralds a time where you may be more forthright and determined than usual. Others may perceive you as driven or argumentative. There may be a moment today where you need to assert your authority with a family member, and this can disturb you.

Thursday 16th

As the Moon meets Pluto in your family sector, you may find that there's some subtle manipulation going on around you. This may not be as tough as it sounds but you might be asked to do something you would rather not. This afternoon you are happier to oblige.

Friday 17th

Today there's tricky energy for you to navigate. You desire to express yourself be it in art, words or by switching up your home environment. Be warned that this may not go to plan as you may have overlooked some rules and regulations. Read the manual before attempting DIY.

Saturday 18th

Reaching out to others and connecting with the world will do you good today. You may come across a wise person who you can learn from. You may also feel triggered by this person who may challenge you to think outside the box and see things differently.

Sunday 19th

Use this peaceful energy to merge lovingly with whatever uplifts you. You may wish to try some time in solitude or spiritual practice. The mysteries of life draw you and you may surprise yourself with your ability to assimilate new concepts. Be good to yourself and enjoy some luxurious time alone.

Monday 20th

A glorious Full Moon in your health and duties sector will highlight your part in the collective. This is a sensitive placement but one which helps you to realise why you are here, what is your purpose and which dream is worth chasing. Surrender to whatever life has in store for you.

Tuesday 21st

Your relationships are on your mind today as you desire to make plans and get active. The Moon's opposition to Mars in your sign can mean that you need another to take the initiative. You may also need to relinquish your need for harmony and let yourself be led.

Wednesday 22nd

Today the Sun enters your sign. This is your birthday month. Happy birthday! It also means that it's the Autumn equinox and day and night are equal lengths. Take this opportunity to centre yourself before the balance tips and the shorter days and longer nights arrive.

Thursday 23rd

You may feel extra balanced and harmonic. Be careful not to upset this by speaking your mind to those who are not accepting. Venus and Uranus are in opposition and for you, this may mean that money matters or an indulgent spend needs attention. You may have tipped your bank balance.

Friday 24th

As the Moon now sits with Uranus, it's likely that your emotions are unstable. You could be regretting a recent purchase and trying to resolve this. Use this volatile energy to come up with something new and innovative instead of mourning a mistake that can't be undone.

Saturday 25th

Tomorrow Mercury will turn retrograde in your sign. Take time today to make sure that all your travel plans are in order and your technical devices are backed up. Mercury may turn things on their head but remember that this is temporary and helps you slow down and contemplate matters.

Sunday 26th

Mercury is now retrograde. Besides this dreaded time, other celestial aspects favour a good day. Mars in your sign will keep things moving forward and the Sun will help to throw light on important issues that Mercury is meddling with. Keep alert as this can be a fruitful time if you allow it.

Monday 27th

Today may be a time where you are over-taxed and need a rest. It may not be possible to see where you're going, and this will frustrate you. Take things slowly and tackle one job at a time. Connect with people only if absolutely necessary.

Tuesday 28th

This morning you may still feel in demand and drained. By afternoon you'll know just what you need to feel safe and nourished again. A work colleague may provide a safe space, or a deadline may be extended giving you time to breathe and relax. Accept help if offered.

Wednesday 29th

Your energy may be low today, but you may still be productive. Your Libran Sun connects to Saturn and they help you get the minimum done. Venus and Neptune are allowing you to enjoy some self-indulgence to wind down this evening. A scented bath may be just the thing.

Thursday 30th

There's a huge amount of watery energy around today. You may be tempted to wallow in self-pity or be seduced by Venus asking you to be good to yourself. Let no-one tell you how to use this energy as you need to nourish your body and soul today.

117

OCTOBER
. . . .

Friday 1st

Fiery energy arrives in time for the weekend and some social time. You may be out and about with your friends or having lively chats with online groups. The Moon makes great connections to the Sun and Mars in your sign making you outreaching and excitable. However, don't neglect family duties.

Saturday 2nd

Seductive Venus asks that you make some changes in your home environment. You could be re-decorating or finding a new avenue to raise extra cash. Adding an exotic touch to your furnishings or even getting a haircut will be influenced under this potent energy and will surely surprise people.

Sunday 3rd

Taking rest time and sorting through your inner filing cabinet will satisfy you today. You need to stay away from drama that doesn't include you as Mercury is causing mischief. He connects to Jupiter in your creative sector, this could get messy. With Jupiter involved, it could be huge.

Monday 4th

Today you may be yearning to get back on track and make solid plans. There's still a lot of thinking to be done and you must learn to be less emotionally attached. Neptune may be charming you away right now but stay in your safety zone and do more research.

Tuesday 5th

The Moon drops back into your sign. You will feel pleased with any changes you have recently made as they bring you joy and comfort. Feminine wisdom is available for you so seek it out via elders in the family who have had a similar experience.

Wednesday 6th

A New Moon in your sign is the best opportunity you have to make goals and intentions regarding your own self and what you desire for you alone. You will be energised today. Check every detail twice as Mercury sits with this Moon. Don't act yet. Pluto also turns direct now.

Thursday 7th

Venus enters your communications sector and will help you to reach out and reconnect with old friends and acquaintances. She may even introduce you to people from foreign lands. You may have intense feelings or secrets that you're holding tightly this afternoon. Be bold and share with someone close.

Friday 8th

The Sun and Mars are combining to make a powerhouse of energy for you to access and use for your New Moon intentions. Any restrictions you may have had will slowly be released and you'll be free to implement your goals. Try not to raise your emotions too high today.

Saturday 9th

You're now back in touch with your direction in life. You may wish to take some time to look around and see what's new here. Mercury is in the heart of the Sun and will receive new downloads for you. Watch for signposts and listen to messages.

Sunday 10th

Saturn turns direct today. This is good news as it means that your creative projects have been given the once over and you're now good to go. You have a lot to do but you do it with grace, high energy and a smile on your face.

Monday 11th

Keep that fire burning inside you. You need to begin implementing your goals and continue getting rid of old thought processes and conditioning. Today will be filled with activity and you may get some inspiration from a leader or elder type figure. Family responsibilities call you this evening.

Tuesday 12th

Today is fairly quiet but does give you a chance to make some of your plans and dreams solid. The Moon gives you ambition and possibly an action plan. This will be enhanced by a connection to Uranus who will have some bright, new ways of achieving these goals. Sudden insights are possible.

Wednesday 13th

As the Moon meets newly direct Pluto you may notice what has been transformed in your family life over the last few months. If this is in line with your own aspirations, then keep doing what you have been doing as it's clearly working. Chatty Venus helps you convince a sceptical person.

Thursday 14th

Saturn now greets the Moon and together they set boundaries and rules that will protect your creative interests now. This can include love interests as Venus is involved here too. You may feel awkward discussing these issues but it's necessary for your personal growth and will ultimately bring you balance.

Friday 15th

Today it would be a good idea if you could get some professional advice from someone who has your best interests at heart. Your ego and emotions are in sync so use this helpful energy to ask around and reach out to others. Friends in your wider circle may help.

Saturday 16th

This is a peaceful day where you get a chance to do something just for you. If helping others is on the agenda, then this will also satisfy. If you have free time, choose an activity where you can switch off and relax. Merging and connecting with spirit will satisfy.

Sunday 17th

Jupiter turns direct today. Things are starting to turn around for you and you will see this happen quickly and in a big way. Many great connections to the Moon help you to sift through your duties with a smile and use the evening to dream.

Monday 18th

Mercury turns direct now too. This is great news as you will have the chance to go over old ground and make sure that you've understood new things. This is the time to assimilate the lessons of the year's retrogrades. Action can begin and you may do this with a partner.

Tuesday 19th

Be very careful that you don't fall out with an important person. Picking up the pieces after Mercury retrograde may mean an apology or two is in order. Mars in your sign may make you overly assertive and pushy. Back away if you see that something troublesome is brewing.

Wednesday 20th

The Full Moon in your relationship sector can show you what has been building in the last six months. What have you achieved here? You may feel the tension building throughout the day and get on the defensive. Use this restless energy to produce something and not destroy it.

Thursday 21st

Unsettled energy continues to grip you as the Moon meets disruptive Uranus. It may be a good idea if you choose to stay alone today as there may be trouble brewing. Try to do something physical and disperse this energy. Good food or a walk in nature will also help.

Friday 22nd

Today you may be stubborn and refuse to make allowances or compromises. It's either your way or the highway. How does this make you feel? If you can see things from the other's perspective, you may regain that sense of equilibrium which is your default setting but lost today.

Saturday 23rd

The Sun enters your finance and values sector where you'll be forced to bring some things out of the shadow and decide how much joy they bring you. This is the time to transform, declutter and get rid. You will see those dark corners more clearly now.

Sunday 24th

In your travel sector, the Moon makes you feel undecided and inconsistent. You can't stick to one way of thinking today. Find someone to talk to and see if you can brainstorm as to why you feel like this. You may simply need to know more facts and figures before making a decision.

Monday 25th

You may have more energy today. In fact, it may be boundless. You may have been saved from drifting into a time of self-loathing and have suddenly bobbed back up into life. Use this spare energy well and look further afield to other cultures and philosophies.

Tuesday 26th

You're sensitive and may be protecting or defending your boundaries. This may well be occurring in the workplace where you normally feel nurtured or the parent figure. It may be difficult to communicate from the heart today so don't try. Leave it until this energy passes.

Wednesday 27th

Today can be very difficult if you're still hiding away from possible attacks. You may see control issues or power struggles between men and women. This may also manifest as conflict between home and work. Stand your ground, you're the best at mediating and can solve this problem with tact and diplomacy.

Thursday 28th

If you're still defending your corner, then today you may get more aggressive. This will not do you any favours. By the time the Moon shifts into your social sector you may be more fired up and self-righteous. Come back to your centre and find your empathy and understanding for all.

Friday 29th

Use all your powers of seeing both sides today and try to come to a happy medium before the weekend. This will unsettle you and you may feel resentful but will be your best option. Mercury in your sign will help you to communicate your feelings more effectively today.

Saturday 30th

Mars leaves your sign after causing some bother over the last week. In your finance and values sector, he will help you to rejuvenate home projects that are dead in the water. You may also see a change in your financial situation. He will bring an ending but also a new beginning.

Sunday 31st

Be at peace. You should use the day to gather your thoughts and throw away those which have done you no service recently. Go through your inner filing cabinet and look for your new coping mechanisms. Whatever surfaces now is doing so to be healed.

NOVEMBER
· · · · · · · · · · · · · · · · ·

Monday 1st

The Moon is in your sign today and your outward appearance is one that's perfectly balanced. Others may need your influence in their lives more. A healthy connection to Pluto means that you can look at change, endings or issues within your family with clarity and discernment.

Tuesday 2nd

Today you may receive guidance from a teacher or an elder in your wider groups. You may learn more about boundaries and how you can still merge with the world and stay protected. Mercury and Pluto square off and can cause some harsh words spoken in your family environment.

Wednesday 3rd

The Moon meets Mercury in your sign. You may find that you have a head full of chatter and emotional attachment surfaces. What you need to get off your chest may not be easy but is necessary for your family members to know where they stand. This will be tricky so stay strong.

Thursday 4th

There's a New Moon in your finances and value sector. Mars and Saturn are involved so it's likely that you are making resolutions regarding money. This is the time to look at taxes, investments and shared finances as there is a shift that needs to happen now.

Friday 5th

Venus is now in your family sector. While she's here you will
see that your ability to be compassionate and discerning is
at its best. Mercury flies into your finance and value sector;
negotiating will be easier now. The energy can be volatile today
so watch out for falling debris and try not to get involved with
any potential explosions.

Saturday 6th

This weekend may be filled with messages, emails and visits
to people you haven't seen for some time. Reminiscing about
the past with siblings or cousins can be fun, but don't get lost
in the past at the expense of the present. There may be an
underlying theme of discussing finances running through your
family commitments right now. This will be important.

Sunday 7th

There's no time for dreaming today, there's too much for you
to do. Your mood is mostly optimistic and upbeat however,
and you whistle while you work. Jupiter is connecting to make
everything bigger. His other influence as law-bringer or priest
may inspire you to be more spiritual or conventional than
usual. Which way will it be for you?

Monday 8th

Today is almost certainly going to involve money talk of
some kind. The Moon meets Venus who loves money whilst
connecting to planets in sectors concerned with values and
shared finances. You may find that an investment or a joint
venture is reaping rewards. Check nothing is overdue, or you
may be in trouble. Now is not the time to bury your head in
the sand and hope it all blows over.

Tuesday 9th

You may be coming a little closer to reaching your dreams now. It's wise to have moments where you contemplate rather than act and today is a day for looking at what needs to be left behind. Pluto asks that you make space for something new.

Wednesday 10th

This is a very tricky day to navigate. Once more, finances, secrets and legacies involving a large group are involved. People will need to toe the line and own their responsibilities now. You may discover something that has been hidden for a long time. Expect heated discussions.

Thursday 11th

You may be speaking your truth in a way that upsets others today. Jupiter hosts the Moon making your emotions larger than they should be. Don't become conceited or a bully. Your home and self-worth may be threatened but this is just your perception. Get all the facts before you act out.

Friday 12th

Don't become a scapegoat and do another's bidding just to keep the peace. You get a glimpse of your true north today and desire to follow on with your path but feel restricted by others. Peace may be achieved if you act as a collective and not an individual.

Saturday 13th

Today it's imperative that you're extremely patient. If you can do this, you'll see more co-operation from others. Mercury and Mars show that the potential for conflict is there, but you're able to use directed energy and speak plainly to prevent this from surfacing.

Sunday 14th

Stay connected to those who matter to you but also take time to meditate or just have some peace. Self-control is important now as others are looking to you to guide them through a difficult time. Fill your cup before handing it out to those in need of your light.

Monday 15th

Support from a partner is much appreciated today. You remember to respect personal boundaries as do they. Family time may have to wait as you need this support for yourself right now. Be respectful and ask people to let you have some space to recharge. Tell them you will be there for them again soon.

Tuesday 16th

Money matters will require your attention. This may cause you some grief and you may not have the energy to deal with it but there are people around you who will. Use them. It's possible that you will need legal advice or help from another professional.

Wednesday 17th

Mars sits opposite Uranus meaning that where finances are concerned there may be trouble or shocks. This will involve several people and you will not be dealing with it alone. Take some time this evening to ground yourself and shake off any negativity that the day has brought.

Thursday 18th

The Moon joins Uranus today and you're highly emotional. There will be a lot you need to say and do, and you may be drained of your energy. Neptune is holding you together and asking that you switch off and consider your own needs today. Take time for yourself.

Friday 19th

A Full Moon in your intimacy sector will highlight recent troubles regarding shared finances. Things may have come to a head and you may be able to come to an agreement. Mark this as a completion of something that has been outstanding for some time. Make room for the new.

Saturday 20th

Your mind is so full that you may not be able to focus today. It may be impossible for you to think and form opinions so wait until you have clarity. You're reaching out and so it may be helpful for you to talk to an elder or professional person.

Sunday 21st

If you try to stay optimistic today, help may come from unlikely sources. Your inner compass is swaying from one side to the other and your true north seems nowhere in sight. Stay calm as this influence is short-lived. Listen to the wise words of a person you admire.

Monday 22nd

The week begins with the Moon in your career sector. You may still be feeling sensitive and touchy. The Sun moves into your communication sector and you will be uplifted if you catch up with people you may have neglected recently. Male and female relationships are looking harmonised and balanced today.

Tuesday 23rd

You may be pleasantly surprised at who comes to your aid
today. Your family and work duties may feel compromised so
do what nurtures you, even if that is helping out someone
in need. One step at a time will get you through the day. Put
money aside for your dreams.

Wednesday 24th

Conflicting interests may cause you to retreat from some
of your duties and obligations this morning. However, by
afternoon you'll have more energy and desire to make your
mark in the world. Mercury enters your communications
sector and helps you research or investigate travel or higher
education studies.

Thursday 25th

Mars and Venus are making a nice connection today. If you
use this energy wisely, you may have a romantic time which
satisfies both parties. Your wider groups will be supportive
if you wish to express something out of the ordinary. Just be
mindful to respect the rules and regulations.

Friday 26th

You may experience some conflict with a leader. Your
self-expression may need to be tailored depending on the
listener. Remember that you're in your interest groups to
learn and grow and not to challenge the existing order.
Someone may pull you aside and remind you of this.

Saturday 27th

This weekend the Moon is in your hidden sector and the best thing you can do is to switch off and rest. You may be called upon to make weekend visits and do chores, but you resist. This is okay. Allow yourself to have some downtime to process your thoughts.

Sunday 28th

You appear to have lost sight of your dreams again and this unsettles you. This is because Neptune is asking you to be patient and relax. Everything will happen when you're aligned and ready to go. For now, be content to enjoy a day of rest and recuperation.

Monday 29th

This morning the Moon drops into your sign and you may feel like your normal self again. This doesn't mean that you must spring into action. It means that your mental faculties are more inclined to find balance. Listen, discern and justify what you hear today.

Tuesday 30th

Your ruler, Venus, is chatting to Neptune today. This influence can help you to realise that dreams are achieved one step at a time. Rushing will make you miss important steps. Conversations with an elder or boss may give you some insight on the which steps you need to take.

DECEMBER

. . . .

Wednesday 1st

Neptune turns direct and you may now begin to get a clear sight of your direction for this part of your life. You're feeling more upbeat and willing to tackle things you have found taxing recently. This will likely include finances or changes that have been made.

Thursday 2nd

You may be ruthless and surprise a few people. You have goals and nothing is going to get in the way of completing them. It's possible that you may start with looking at your home environment or your bank balance and giving both a makeover.

Friday 3rd

The Moon meets Mars in your finance and values sector. Your energy will be high and directed. People need to get out of your path now as you steamroller your way through the day. This afternoon you may be ticking off your 'to do' list and this will please you greatly.

Saturday 4th

There is a New Moon in your communications sector. This is a good time to set goals and intentions that will help you achieve your dreams or part of them. First, you need to reconcile your attachment to old dreams and let them go with love and gratitude as they have sustained you up until now.

Sunday 5th

You have great optimism and finally see the steps you must take to make your dreams a reality. Family issues may need your attention. Show your leadership qualities and let family members know that you're there for them no matter what, but you have your own life too.

Monday 6th

The energy today is good for spending on little changes that will be long lasting. This could be a change in your home or the way you look. You may keep people guessing as they are wondering what you're up to. Surprise yourself with doing something out of character for you.

Tuesday 7th

You know in your heart that change is good. As a Libran you may fear change as it upsets your equilibrium but deep down you understand that without change there is no growth. This afternoon you reach out to those you consider your tribe.

Wednesday 8th

Today may be tricky as you find that you're up against leaders or authority figures who may trigger you. Remember that triggers are meant to help you understand yourself better. Keep healthy boundaries in place and express your own needs today even if it upsets someone else. Put yourself first.

Thursday 9th

Your creative expression may be on the edge of taboo or risqué topics today. You may be reprimanded about this and told to back off. This afternoon would be a good time to pause and reflect on your new-found boisterous attitude. Is it really helping you make progress?

Friday 10th

Use today for some quiet meditation and for thinking outside the box. You may have some duties and obligations to get through but when there's spare time, disconnect and be alone. Merging with spirit or your ideals will calm you and bring you back in alignment with your own true self.

Saturday 11th

The Moon meets Neptune who acts as your inner compass. Surrender to your thoughts and allow yourself to dream. Make a vision board if you can. Venus also meets Pluto today and you may see some subtle manipulation going on in your home environment. If this doesn't involve you, stay away.

Sunday 12th

Passive-aggressive behaviour may make its way into your family. Venus and Pluto can be a tricky influence to manage. Women will want their own way. This may simply be that upcoming holiday arrangements are being discussed and there's disagreement going on. Be patient and mediate if you need to.

Monday 13th

Mercury moves into your family sector. He will help with negotiations and maintaining peace talks. Your leadership skills will be noticed now. Mars also shifts signs and marches into your communication sector. You can expect to be more assertive and direct now. Tell it like it is.

Tuesday 14th

Your personal relationships and romantic interests may be at odds with your family needs. It may be difficult to manage these areas of life. There's much to do and you prefer that your partner takes the lead or helps. Make plans and stick to them.

Wednesday 15th

The Moon meets Uranus in your intimacy sector. You can expect that your emotions will get stirred up and you may need to put your foot down with someone. If you need to take an authoritative stance then do so by being mindful of personal boundaries, yours and others.

Thursday 16th

The grounding energy today can help you feel back in touch with your daily routines. The festivities are growing closer and you'll need to be on top of your game. If you're not feeling it, try some yoga, meditation or a walk outdoors. Good food and company will help too.

Friday 17th

You may have a lot going on in your mind and will try to sort out what's more important. However, your energy is drained, and you would rather watch a good film. You're drawn to other cultures, but you may be using this as a distraction.

Saturday 18th

It's possible that you have a moment of crisis and doubt that you will ever be able to attain your dreams. This is just a passing phase as there are other things that are more pressing, and you may be resisting doing them. Go with the flow.

Sunday 19th

Venus turns retrograde. Over the next forty days you may see old family issues or lovers from the past come back. There may be permanent endings to deal with. A Full Moon also appears in your travel sector. Look at what you have achieved over the last six months.

Monday 20th

You may be feeling very sensitive to criticism. The stress accompanied with this season may be affecting you. If you need to get around a particular problem, especially involving work, try thinking outside the box and you may find an innovative solution and surprise a few people.

Tuesday 21st

The Winter Solstice arrives. This is the longest night and things may seem a little gloomy. You're protective of the work you have done this year and may be on the defensive. Let it drop and enjoy this long, dark night where you can contemplate the year gone by.

Wednesday 22nd

What you need is some fun with friends. There may a festive social gathering which will lift your spirits and raise your energy levels. It's possible that you bump into someone who annoys you as they're too uptight and strict. You may coax them to let their hair down and relax.

Thursday 23rd

Jupiter returns to the very end of your creative sector. If you have words of love to profess, do it now as they will be warmly received. A creative project may be begging to be finished while you have the energy. You will shine today.

Friday 24th

If it's possible, steal some time to organise your thoughts and get rid of some mess. Get out your internal planner and ensure that you have made time for everyone over the festive season. Today may be draining and hard on you. Play by the rules and toe the line.

Saturday 25th

Venus retrograde meets Pluto again. You may see this influencing your family and power struggles will surface. Make sure that there's not one person doing all the work for this festive day. Working as a group will be more beneficial and help you enjoy the day together.

Sunday 26th

You are able to be of service to someone who is struggling today. This may be by offering physical help or simply listening to their woes. Mercury and Neptune connect, and you find yourself sharing your dreams and visions to people willing to listen. You're on top form this evening.

Monday 27th

Today you may enjoy a quieter time and you're able to unwind. Your personal energy will return and you will want to follow your own agenda. Let others know that this is what you plan to do as you may have some objections from people expecting you to be in attendance.

Tuesday 28th

The Moon in your sign connects to Mercury, Venus and Pluto in your family sector. Although you may try to disconnect and do your own thing, you still have to be a part of the tribe. This may cause you some grief and knock your energy levels back down again.

Wednesday 29th

Jupiter enters your health and duties sector for the next twelve months. You may enjoy a boost of good health or joy in serving others now. An intense Moon sits opposite Uranus pushing your emotions close to the edge. If you need to erupt, remove yourself from others.

Thursday 30th

Mercury meets Pluto today and they have a talk about Mercury's next mission for you. This will involve your role in the family and your roots. You may see a ghost from the past now and this can be a pleasant experience. Be on your best behaviour as you're being observed.

Friday 31st

The end of the year is here, and your energy is high. You're raring to get out and enjoy more celebrations. If you find yourself looking back on the year, remember to pull out the good bits and not to focus on the bad. Have fun this evening.

Libra

· · · · · · · · · · · · · · · ·

PEOPLE WHO SHARE
YOUR SIGN

PEOPLE WHO SHARE YOUR SIGN

....

For decades, Librans have been the zodiac's providers of balance and beauty. From famous lawyers such as Judge Judy to fashion designers such as Ralph Lauren, Librans can be fair and fashionable. Whether they blow fans away with their talents or raise friends up with their Positive energy, they are sure to charm themselves into the hearts of many. Discover the Librans who share your exact birthday and see if you can spot the similarities.

24th September

Pia Wurtzbach (1989), Kimberley Nixon (1985), Stephanie McMahon (1976), Jackie Sandler (1974), Kevin Sorbo (1958), Phil Hartman (1948), Jim Henson (1936), F. Scott Fitzgerald (1896)

25th September

Donald Glover (1983), Declan Donnelly (1975), Catherine Zeta-Jones (1969), Will Smith (1968), Keely Shaye Smith (1963), Heather Locklear (1961), Michael Madsen (1957), Christopher Reeve (1952), Mark Hamill (1951), Michael Douglas (1944), William Faulkner (1897)

26th September

Lilly Singh (1988), Talulah Riley (1985), Nev Schulman (1984), Jón Richardson (1982), Christina Milian (1981), Serena Williams (1981), Petro Poroshenko, Ukrainian President (1965), Olivia Newton-John (1948), Martin Heidegger (1889), T. S. Eliot (1888)

27th September

Simona Halep (1991), Lola Kirke (1990), Avril Lavigne (1984), Anna Camp (1982), Lil Wayne (1982), Carrie Brownstein (1974), Gwyneth Paltrow (1972), Marc Maron (1963)

28th September

Hilary Duff (1987), St. Vincent (1982), Bam Margera (1979), Naomi Watts (1968), Mira Sorvino (1967), Brigitte Bardot (1934), Bhagat Singh (1907)

29th September

Halsey (1994), Kevin Durant (1988), Dani Pedrosa (1985), Zachary Levi (1980), Roger Bart (1962), Ian McShane (1942), Jerry Lee Lewis (1935)

30th September

Levi Miller (2002), Maddie Ziegler (2002), Max Verstappen (1997), Ezra Miller (1992), Olivier Giroud (1986), Lacey Chabert (1982), Kieran Culkin (1982), Marion Cotillard (1975), Monica Bellucci (1964)

1st October

Brie Larson (1989), Matthew Daddario (1987), Sarah Drew (1980), Zach Galifianakis (1969), Theresa May (1956), André Rieu (1949), Julie Andrews (1935), George Peppard (1928), Jimmy Carter, U.S. President (1924)

2nd October

Camilla Belle (1986), Kelly Ripa (1970), Lorraine Bracco (1954), Sting (1951), Annie Leibovitz (1949), Donna Karan (1948), Don McLean (1945), Johnnie Cochran (1937), Groucho Marx (1890), Mahatma Gandhi (1869)

3rd October

Alicia Vikander (1988), Ashlee Simpson (1984), Tessa Thompson (1983), Seann William Scott (1976), Neve Campbell (1973), Lena Headey (1973), Gwen Stefani (1969), Clive Owen (1964), Al Sharpton (1954), Yohji Yamamoto (1943)

4th October

Dakota Johnson (1989), Stacey Solomon (1989), Melissa Benoist (1988), Caitriona Balfe (1979), Alicia Silverstone (1976), Liev Schreiber (1967), Christoph Waltz (1956), Susan Sarandon (1946), Charlton Heston (1923)

5th October

Jacob Tremblay (2006), Jesse Eisenberg (1983), Nicky Hilton (1983), Kate Winslet (1975), Guy Pearce (1967), Bernie Mac (1957), Imran Khan, Pakistani Prime Minister (1952), Bob Geldof (1951)

6th October

Jazz Jennings (2000), Olivia Thirlby (1986), Jeremy Sisto (1974), Ioan Gruffudd (1973), Romero Britto (1963), Elisabeth Shue (1963), Britt Ekland (1942), Jerry Heller (1940)

7th October

Kira Kosarin (1997), Diego Costa (1988), Holland Roden (1986), Alesha Dixon (1978), Thom Yorke (1968), Toni Braxton (1967), Simon Cowell (1959)

8th October

Bella Thorne (1997), Barbara Palvin (1993), Bruno Mars (1985), Travis Pastrana (1983), Nick Cannon (1980), Matt Damon (1970), Anne-Marie Duff (1970), Sigourney Weaver (1949), Chevy Chase (1943), R.L. Stine (1943), Jesse Jackson (1941), Paul Hogan (1939)

9th October

Bella Hadid (1996), Tyler James Williams (1992), Chris O'Dowd (1979), Brandon Routh (1979), David Cameron (1966), Scott Bakula (1954), Sharon Osbourne (1952), Jackson Browne (1948), John Lennon (1940)

10th October

Xherdan Shaqiri (1991), Marina and the Diamonds (1985), Dan Stevens (1982), Mario Lopez (1973), Wendi McLendon-Covey (1969), Tanya Tucker (1958), David Lee Roth (1954), Nora Roberts (1950), Charles Dance (1946)

11th October

Michelle Trachtenberg (1985), Bradley James (1983), Matt Bomer (1977), Emily Deschanel (1976), Jane Krakowski (1968), Luke Perry (1966), Joan Cusack (1962), Dawn French (1957), Fred Trump (1905), Eleanor Roosevelt (1884)

12th October

Josh Hutcherson (1992), Calum Scott (1988), Tyler Blackburn (1986), Katie Piper (1983), Hugh Jackman (1968), Hiroyuki Sanada (1960), Luciano Pavarotti (1935)

13th October

Tiffany Trump (1993), Ashanti (1980), David Haye (1980),
Sacha Baron Cohen (1971), Kate Walsh (1967), Kelly Preston
(1962), Beverly Johnson (1952), Paul Simon (1941), Margaret
Thatcher (1925)

14th October

Rowan Blanchard (2001), Lourdes Leon (1996), Usher (1978),
Natalie Maines (1974), Steve Coogan (1965), Cliff Richard (1940),
Ralph Lauren (1939), Roger Moore (1927), E. E. Cummings
(1894), Dwight D. Eisenhower, U.S. President (1890)

15th October

Anthony Joshua (1989), Mesut Özil (1988), Keyshia Cole (1981),
Dominic West (1969), Tanya Roberts (1955), Richard Carpenter
(1946), A. P. J. Abdul Kalam, Indian President (1931), Friedrich
Nietzsche (1844)

16th October

Naomi Osaka (1997), John Mayer (1977), Davina McCall (1967),
Flea (1962), Tim Robbins (1958), Angry Grandpa (1950), Angela
Lansbury (1925), Oscar Wilde (1854)

17th October

Felicity Jones (1983), Kimi Räikkönen (1979), Matthew
Macfadyen (1974), Eminem (1972), Ziggy Marley (1968), Evel
Knievel (1938), Rita Hayworth (1918), Arthur Miller (1915)

18th October

Tyler Posey (1991), Zac Efron (1987), Freida Pinto (1984), Ne-Yo (1979), Jean-Claude Van Damme (1960), Martina Navratilova (1956), Chuck Berry (1926), Pierre Trudeau, Canadian Prime Minister (1919)

19th October

Hunter King (1993), Rebecca Ferguson (1983), Gillian Jacobs (1982), Desmond Harrington (1976), Trey Parker (1969), Jon Favreau (1966), John Lithgow (1945), Michael Gambon (1940)

20th October

Jess Glynne (1989), Candice Swanepoel (1988), John Krasinski (1979), Snoop Dogg (1971), Dannii Minogue (1971), Si King (1967), Viggo Mortensen (1958), Danny Boyle (1956), James Chadwick (1891)

21st October

Kim Kardashian (1980), Glen Powell (1988), Amber Rose (1983), Andrew Scott (1976), Ken Watanabe (1959), Carrie Fisher (1956), Patti Davis (1952), Benjamin Netanyahu, Israeli Prime Minister (1949), Judy Sheindlin "Judge Judy" (1942), Alfred Nobel (1833)

22nd October

Corey Hawkins (1988), Deontay Wilder (1985), Spike Jonze (1969), Shaggy (1968), Bob Odenkirk (1962), Jeff Goldblum (1952), Arsène Wenger (1949), Deepak Chopra (1946), Christopher Lloyd (1938), Franz Liszt (1811)

. . . .

23rd October

Amandla Stenberg (1998), Ireland Baldwin (1995), Jessica Stroup (1986), Izabel Goulart (1984), Cat Deeley (1976), Ryan Reynolds (1976), "Weird Al" Yankovic (1959), Martin Luther King III (1957), Ang Lee (1954), Pelé (1940)